BOOK D
READING FOR CONCEPTS

"All things change; nothing perishes."   Ovid

WILLIAM LIDDLE

General Editor
Director, Instructional Services
Colorado Springs Public Schools
Director of the Reading Clinic, the Colorado College
Colorado Springs, Colorado

BOOK D READING

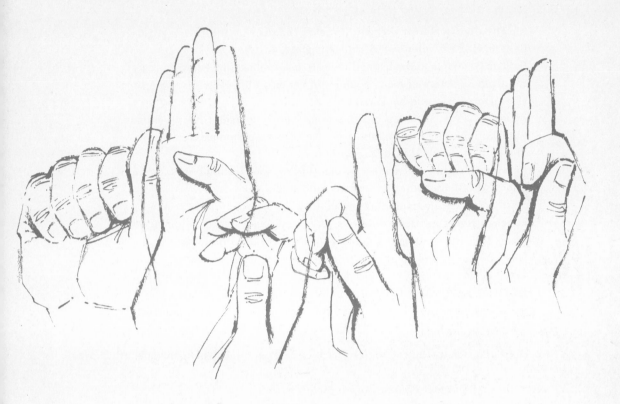

FOR CONCEPTS
Second Edition

WEBSTER DIVISION
McGRAW-HILL BOOK COMPANY

New York   St. Louis   San Francisco
Aukland   Bogotá   Düsseldorf   Johannesburg   London   Madrid
Mexico   Montreal   New Delhi   Panama   Paris   São Paulo
Singapore   Sydney   Tokyo   Toronto

Contributing Authors for the Reading for Concepts Series:

Linda Barton, feature writer for *St. Louis Today.*
Roberta H. Berry, elementary school teacher, writer.
Barbara Broeking, journalist and educational publications editor.
Eth Clifford, author of many volumes of fiction and poetry for youth.
Ellen Dolan, juvenile book author.
Barbara R. Frey, Professor of Education, State University College, Buffalo, N.Y.
Ruth Harley, author and editor of young people's periodicals.
Phyllis W. Kirk, children's book editor.
Richard Kirk, author of science, social studies, and reading books for youth.
Thomas D. Mantel, attorney and juvenile author.
Marilyn F. Peachin, journalist and editor.
James N. Rogers, author-editor of science and social studies resource books.
James J. Pflaum, author and editor of current events periodicals.
Gloria S. Rosenzweig, writer of primary teaching materials.
Jean Shirley, author of juvenile books.
Rosemary Winebrenner, editor of children's books.
Jean White, journalist and writer of young people's reference materials.

Educational Consultant:

Dr. Ruth Gallant, The Center for Teaching and Learning, University of North Dakota, Grand Forks, N.D.

Statisticians for Original Prepublication Field Trials:

Dr. Michael Grady and Dr. Roslyn Grady, Colorado Springs, Colo.
Robert Hampson, Pupil Accounting and Testing Services, Colorado Springs, Colo.

Resource Committee:

Ruth Liddle, Eleanor Wier, Ruth Mitchell, Jean Keeley, and Joseph Tockman.

Project Editor: Carol Washburne
Designer: Jim Darby
Editing Supervisor: Sal Allocco
Production Supervisor: Karen Romano

Illustrators: James Cummings; Tony Giamis, GAI
Cover Photo: NASA

ISBN 0-07-037664-6

TABLE OF CONTENTS

Purpose

This book is one of eight in the series "Reading for Concepts." It was designed to provide an opportunity for young readers to grow in reading experience while exploring a wide variety of ideas contained in several of the academic disciplines.

Three basic underlying concepts are reflected within this book. They are: *Different patterns of life are found in the world, Different communities need and use different ways to reach the same goals,* and *Communities establish patterns of behavior.* The overriding concept in this book is ways in which things organize to allow for change.

To illustrate these concepts, stories have been written around intriguing pieces of information which reflect these ideas. The content has been drawn from the eight disciplines of history, biology, economics, sociology, art, geography, engineering, and anthropology. In this way a wide array of content for meeting various interests has been assured.

Three stories are presented in each discipline. A narrative follows after stories 24, 48, and 72. The narratives, largely drawn from folk literature, will provide a change of pace and are "just for fun" types of stories.

Teaching Procedure

The child will be given a diagnostic test at the beginning of the program to help the teacher determine at which reading level he or she should be placed.

1. Discuss the title and picture clue in the story and establish purposes for reading it.

2. Present difficult words in advance. (There is an index at the back of this book which will direct the teacher in selecting the words expected to cause difficulties at each reading level.)

3. Have students read the story silently. A timed approach may be useful. The stories are all approximately 200 words long. Narratives lengths are listed. Begin with a reading time suitable to the average needs of the group. Moderate speed in reading is an indication of reading proficiency, but it is not the basic province of this series. As comprehension increases, the emphasis may switch to reducing reading time. At this time, use a stopwatch and figure each reader's rate for a story and encourage reading more quickly each subsequent time. By using the charts the reader can see personal progress.

4. Following each regular story is a test which is especially designed to improve specific skills in reading. There are charts at the end of this book on which to record scores of each skill tested. By carefully using these charts, teacher and pupil can make a diagnosis of specific skill weaknesses and also keep track of progress in each aspect of reading skill.

The sample exercise that begins the pupil's text should be reviewed carefully with all pupils. Each test item in the sample should be examined. Pupils should understand in advance exactly how they are to arrive at correct answers, whether they are expected to retain information, to verify from the text, to find the exact word needed, or to conjecture on the basis of information given. Success is necessary. The sample exercise will be found at the end of this discussion.

The skills tested in Book D are typical of those suggested in Bloom's *Taxonomy of Educational Objectives*. Bloom's Taxonomy is a way of ordering thinking from recall, the simplest thought process, to the most abstract order of thinking, synthesis. A taxonomy is a scale, the use of which is a means of establishing where along a hierarchy of thinking one is operating. The point of the test questions is to build a series of test items that incorporate the range of thinking skills as they are reflected in the Taxonomy.

Item 1. Knowledge of specific facts. The answers here must be selected from a group of possibilities. The correct answer selected from multiple alternatives is a directly stated fact in the story. This retention skill would correspond to Bloom's knowledge category, especially to "Knowledge of Specific Facts." The nature of the articles, of course, contributes to the awareness of some key facts about particular cultures, etc.

Item 2. Recognition of meaning of word in context. The student must choose and write the correct response. This skill corresponds to Bloom's "Knowledge of Terminology," especially to the area of "Familiarity with a large number of words in their common range of meaning."

Item 3. This item is intended to make pupils aware of correct form and usage. The student must select the word, or words, described by the words used in the stem of the question. It may be an adjective, a descriptive phrase, or even the predicate of the sentence. The student must find the necessary word in the story and write it. This skill falls within Bloom's "Knowledge of Conventions."

Item 4. Recognition of implications or inferences. This item requires selecting the correct inference from several choices. The response required comes from a multiple choice of implied details. The skill relates to Bloom's "Extrapolation."

Item 5. Knowledge of specific facts. The answers here must be selected from a group of possibilities. The correct answer selected from multiple alternatives is a directly stated fact in the story. This retention skill would correspond to Bloom's knowledge category, especially to "Knowledge of Specific Facts." The nature of the articles, of course, contributes to the awareness of some key facts about particular cultures, etc.

Item 6. Ability to make substantiation from content. This item requires the reader to reread to prove a point. The reader must determine whether or not the given statement is in the story. This skill is specifically one of attention to the task of reading.

Item 7. Recognition of the meaning of the whole. This item requires the reader to select the answer which best describes the central theme of the story.

This skill corresponds to Bloom's "Meaning of the Whole—Interpretation."

Item 8. This item expects the learner to make an interpretation. The reader must confirm an understanding of the nature of a fact, process, or problem and must select the one response among the given alternatives which most nearly shows the cause, or the meaning, of the stated effect as explained in the story. This item corresponds to Bloom's level two of thinking: "Comprehension."

Item 9. Recognition of implications or inferences. This item requires selecting the correct inference from several choices. The response required comes from a multiple choice of implied details. The skill relates to Bloom's "Extrapolation."

Method

Each story has been written to the specifications for a controlled vocabulary and readability level. The readability level of this book was determined through application of the Dale-Chall Readability Formula. See the manual for statistical information.

Words not in the controlled vocabulary list were limited to words according to standard lists of words suitable for pupils slightly older than their reading level would imply. In some cases, the content required the use of a highly specialized word. Such words are carefully defined by context clues in the story itself and are listed in the index.

Field Testing

In the testing population, a wide range of background and abilities of pupils were represented. See the manual for details. The results of extensive field testing were used to revise the materials until an optimum ease index was achieved. Preliminary practice should be provided. See teaching notes for the practice selection for specific directions necessary to make each question a learning experience.

The teacher should also remind the reader where it is necessary to look back into the story to find answers.

Concept Recapitulations

After pupils have completed the text, the following suggestions may be helpful in conducting a discussion which will tie together the information carried in the individual articles in terms of the overall concept. This type of activity is important not for the particular information pupils will meet in these books but for the beginnings of building a wider view of the human environment. Information from widely divergent fields can interact to contribute to broad, intellectual awareness, whereas most education tends to fracture rather than serve the development of such wide-angle perspective.

Often, those youngsters most resistant to formal educational processing have drawn their own conclusions about the world and how it works. These students, in particular, may take fresh challenge from the experience of using pieces of information as the flexible building blocks for at least one unified meaningful whole. This type of reading is helping them practice the necessary modern skill of "continuous translation." Here skill building in reading has been attached not only to immediate short-range motivation and information accumulation but also to long-range creative reassessment of apparently dissimilar content. Great openness and considerable flexibility will be required from teachers who will make the greatest use of this aspect of this reading program. The possibilities for student growth and awakenings are enormous.

A procedure such as the following is suggested:

"You have read stories about three big ideas. Consider the first idea that *different patterns of life are found in the world.* In the beginning of the book you were asked to keep certain questions in mind. Can you answer these questions now?" (Pupils meet guiding questions on page 13.)

1. Is life the same everywhere?

2. Do other people influence us and the way we live?

3. How do other people's lives differ from yours?

4. Do you think the way you live affects other people?

5. Is it a good thing that there are differences in the way people live?

"The second big idea that you read about was that *different communities need and use different ways to reach the same goals.* Can you now answer the following questions?" (Guide questions are on page 65.)

1. Must everyone approach a problem in the same way?

2. What are some problems that all people have?

3. Can you think of some ways to solve these problems?

4. Would it help if you knew how other people might solve these problems?

5. Why doesn't everyone solve the problem in the same way?

"The third big idea that you read about was that *communities establish patterns of behavior.* Can you now answer the following questions?" (Guide questions are on page 117.)

1. How do customs come about?

2. Do these things happen over a short period of time or over a long period of time?

3. What are some customs that you have?

4. Where do you think these customs came from?

5. Have you been influenced in your customs by the customs of other people?

Have a few priming possibilities ready to suggest, or shape them out of the early offerings from the group. Sophisticated statements and a review of specifics are not to be expected. Look for signs of mental play and the movement of information from one setting to another. It is perfectly reasonable to conclude with unanswered questions for pupils to ponder in retrospect. However, it is important to give pupils the satisfaction of enthusiastic acceptance of their early attempts at this type of open-ended speculation.

A. Turn to page 14. Look at the picture. Read the title. Think about what the story will say.

B. Study the words for this page on the list beginning page 174.

C. Read the story carefully.

D. Put your name and the title of the story on a sheet of paper. Number from one to nine. Begin the test on the page next to the story.

1. This question asks you to remember something the story has told you. Which of the four choices is correct for this sentence?

2. This question asks you to find the word in the story that means the same as the words in italics. The question gives you a paragraph number. Read that part again to be sure you have the right word.

3. Reread the paragraph given. Which word is described by the words given in the question? The given words must modify or explain the noun you select.

4. This question wants you to think about the story. The answer is not in your book. Read the choices. Choose the one that is the very best guess you might make from the ideas you have just read.

5. The question tests your memory for a detail. Which of the choices agrees with the story?

6. The question requires that you confirm whether or not an idea was actually presented in the story you have just read. If the sentence is wrong according to the information, you have just read, choose *No*. If the information was not given at all, be sure to answer *Does not say.*

7. This question asks you to choose a statement about the entire story. Don't select an idea that fits only one small part. Your answer should fit all of the story.

8. The story gives you the information you need. Refer to it again to be sure which of the given choices is the best explanation.

9. On the basis of the story, which of the choices is most likely to be true? The answer is not in the story. You will have to

think about the ideas and draw your own conclusions.

E. Check your work. The answers for the first test are given below. Your teacher may let you use the answer key for other tests. She may check your work for you.

F. Put the number correct at the top of your paper. Now go back and recheck the answers that were wrong. Do you see now how the correct answer was better? How can you get ready to do the next test better?

G. Turn to page 170. The directions tell you how to put your score onto a record chart. Your teacher will tell you if you may write in the book. If not, she will help you make a copy.

Looking for the Big Idea

The first 24 stories in this book lead you to see one big idea which we call a concept. Before each group of 24 stories, there is an opening page. This page asks you a few questions to keep in mind as you read. Think about the way each story might be pointing out the big idea. Do you agree with the idea? Do you find places that suggest it could be wrong?

Just for Fun

Your book has three longer stories that are just for fun. These stories, beginning on pages 62, 114, and 166, are from old folktales. There are no questions to answer.

Answers for Practice Test, page 15

1. c	2. charge	3. Indian stirrup
4. b	5. d	6. No
7. b	8. a	9. b

I

Different Patterns of Life Are Found in the World

In this section you will read about new and different patterns of life that are found in the world. You will read about these things from the standpoint of history, biology, economics, sociology, art, geography, engineering, and anthropology.

Keep these questions in mind when you are reading.

1. How does life in the United States differ from life in Europe?

2. How do different life patterns affect people in our country?

3. Do these differences affect you?

4. Do our life patterns affect people in other countries?

5. Is it good that there are differences in life patterns?

Soldiers in Stirrups

1   A long time ago, soldiers fought wars on foot. Then they began to ride horses to battle. Until the invention of the stirrup, though, men could not fight well with swords or spears while on horseback.

2   Without stirrups, soldiers had no place to put their feet. They could not stand up to use their swords without falling off their horses. They could throw spears only with the force of their arms.

3   Using stirrups, a soldier could stand up in his saddle. He could put a spear under the top part of his arm and charge with the force of his horse. He could use force when fighting with a sword. And he could win most fights against soldiers who did not use stirrups.

4   The first stirrups were made in India. Because the weather was warm, people did not wear shoes. The Indian stirrup was made of rope. It fit around the big toes. Later, the Chinese made a foot stirrup of wood. Because the Chinese lived in a colder country, the stirrup had to fit around shoes. Still later, around A.D. 700, soldiers in Asia used strong iron foot stirrups.

14

1. Stirrups were first made in
   a. China.
   c. India.
   b. Japan.
   d. Korea.

2. The word in paragraph 3 that means *to attack* or *to rush into battle*

   is _____.

3. The words "made of rope" in paragraph 4 tell about the

   _____ _____.

4. The story does not say so, but it makes you think that stirrups were
   invented before
   a. saddles.   b. guns.   c. rope.

5. Around A.D. 700, the soldiers in Asia used stirrups made of
   a. wood.
   c. shoes.
   b. rope.
   d. iron.

6. Wars were first fought on horseback.
   Yes   No   Does not say

7. On the whole, this story is about
   a. the soldiers in warm and cold countries.
   b. an invention that changed man's way of fighting wars.
   c. how to throw a spear.

8. How did the stirrup help soldiers fight better? (Check the story again.)
   a. They could now stand in their saddles to throw spears.
   b. They looked better when they were using stirrups.
   c. Horses were safer.

9. Which of these sentences do you think is right?
   a. There were no wars 2,000 years ago.
   b. Men were fighting 2,000 years ago.
   c. War is something new.

A Different Kind of Beauty

1   Japan is made up of a chain of islands that lie off the coast of Asia. People came to live in Japan from the nearby countries of China and Korea. From these older countries, the Japanese borrowed ideas, inventions, and habits.

2   For many years, the Japanese built buildings like those in China. They dressed like the Chinese. From China came their way of writing and their habit of drinking tea.

3   In more recent times, the Japanese have borrowed from the United States. They have a government like ours. They do much work in science, as we do. Baseball is a favorite sport in Japan, just as it is here.

4   Things change when they come to Japan. The Japanese improve on almost everything they borrow. The art of garden-making came from Korea or China, but Japanese gardens are special. Each garden has a waterfall, a pond, and small bridges. There are few flowers in Japanese gardens. But the gardens are green during all seasons because they have many evergreens. Japanese gardens have a different kind of beauty.

16

1. The Japanese borrowed ideas from
    a. South America.   c. England.
    b. Canada.   d. China.

2. The word in paragraph 4 that means *to make better* is

    _____.

3. The words "green during all seasons" in paragraph 4 describe the

    _____ _____.

4. The story does not say so, but it makes you think that
    a. Japanese gardens are different from Chinese gardens.
    b. Japan is older than China.
    c. the Japanese cannot grow crops because their soil is poor.

5. Each Japanese garden has
    a. many flowers.   c. a pond.
    b. few evergreens.   d. vegetables.

6. Things change when they come to Japan.
    Yes   No   Does not say

7. On the whole, this story is about
    a. the Japanese.   b. tea.   c. clothing.

8. Why do the Japanese change the things that they borrow? (Check the
    story again.)
    a. They don't like them the way they are.
    b. They try to make them better.
    c. They want visitors to like their changes.

9. Which of these sentences do you think is right?
    a. There are few gardens in Japan.
    b. Peoples from many countries came to live in Japan.
    c. The Japanese invented the habit of drinking tea.

The Traveling Alphabet

1   Three thousand years ago, Phoenicia (fə nish′ ə) was one of the small countries along the Mediterranean Sea. The Phoenicians were sailors and traders who rowed in large sailboats to countries along the Mediterranean.

2   They traded goods with other countries. They also traded ideas with the people they met. In their travels, the Phoenicians came across a people who used an alphabet. Alphabetic writing has a letter for each sound.

3   In those days, most writing was made up of signs. The signs stood for whole words. It was hard to remember and to write so many words. The Phoenicians needed a good way to keep business records. With the letters of an alphabet, the Phoenicians could write any word they wanted. They could keep records more easily with the help of their borrowed alphabet.

4   As the Phoenician traders went from country to country, the alphabet traveled with them. Other people liked the idea of using letters, too. Many began to use the same way of writing.

5   In this manner, the alphabet spread to many lands. The letters were changed slowly over the centuries. But the alphabet we use today comes from the one used by the Phoenicians long ago.

18

1. The Phoenician traders traveled in
   - a. rowboats.
   - b. steamboats.
   - c. sailboats.
   - d. clipper ships.

2. The word in paragraph 5 that means *way* or *method* is

   _____.

3. The words "made up of signs" in paragraph 3 describe the word

   _____.

4. The story does not say so, but it makes you think that the Phoenicians
   - a. borrowed records.
   - b. were good businessmen.
   - c. lived on an island.

5. Alphabetic writing uses
   - a. letters.
   - b. signs.
   - c. ideas.
   - d. boats.

6. The Phoenicians learned about an alphabet during their travels.
   Yes   No   Does not say

7. On the whole, this story is about
   - a. sailors.
   - b. Phoenicia.
   - c. an alphabet.

8. Why did the Phoenicians start using an alphabet? (Check the story again.)
   - a. They did not know how to make signs.
   - b. They wanted a better way to keep records.
   - c. They wanted to trade it for valuable goods.

9. Which of these sentences do you think is right?
   - a. An alphabet made writing easier and quicker.
   - b. The Phoenicians rowed their boats around the world.
   - c. The sea was not important to the Phoenicians.

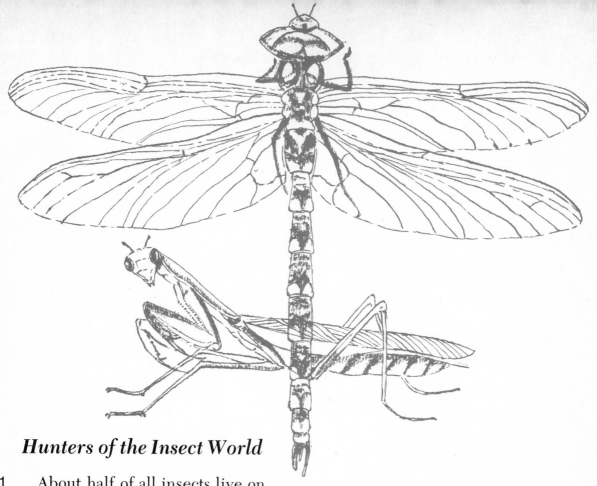

Hunters of the Insect World

1   About half of all insects live on plants. The rest catch and kill other insects for food. They are the hunters of the insect world.

2   Each kind of hunter insect has a weapon. The dragonfly uses its legs as a basket to scoop up other insects. The sand wasp has a stinger it uses to stun its victims.

3   Some hunter insects set traps. The tiger beetle digs a small hole and gets in. Only its head is at the top of the hole. The tiger beetle can pop its head out like a jack-in-the-box. It catches its victims by surprise.

4   The ant lion digs a hole in the sand and waits at the bottom. When an ant or other insect gets near the hole, the sand gives way. The victim slides down into the jaws of the waiting ant lion.

5   The praying mantis is a large insect that looks as if it has arms. Its "arms" are really legs, but they are not used for walking. They are used to grab and hold its victims.

6   We fight to keep down the number of insects that eat our food. Can you see how hunter insects help people?

FIND THE ANSWERS

1. Each kind of hunter insect
   - a. picks a leader.
   - b. has a weapon.
   - c. eats plants.
   - d. has a basket.

2. The word in paragraph 2 that means *to make helpless* is

   _____.

3. The words "looks as if it has arms" in paragraph 5 refer to the

   _____ _____.

4. The story does not say so, but it makes you think that hunter insects
   - a. eat our food.
   - b. are dangerous to people and animals.
   - c. catch insects that damage crops.

5. The dragonfly uses its legs to
   - a. scoop up insects.
   - b. grab insects.
   - c. stab insects.
   - d. sting insects.

6. The tiger beetle is gold with black stripes.

   Yes   No   Does not say

7. On the whole, this story is about
   - a. insects that use stingers.
   - b. insects that hunt other insects.
   - c. ants and lions.

8. What is meant by the sentence, "The tiger beetle can pop its head out like a jack-in-the-box"?
   - a. The tiger beetle makes noises.
   - b. The tiger beetle moves quickly.
   - c. The tiger beetle is funny.

9. Which of these sentences do you think is right?
   - a. About half of all insects are hunter insects.
   - b. People fight the hunter insects.
   - c. All hunter insects dig holes to trap their victims.

A Spider Without a Web

1   Most spiders build webs to trap other insects. But the trap-door spider has another way of hunting. First, she digs a hole about ten inches deep and an inch and a half wide. Next, she makes a lid of dirt and webbing. This trap door must fit over the upper end of the hole like a cork fits in a bottle.

2   Finally, the spider hides her nest by spreading dirt over the lid. Then the trap door looks like the earth around it. Sometimes she even plants moss on top. She is as sly as a fox.

3   The trap-door spider hunts at night. For hours, she stays hidden right below her door. She holds it open just a crack as she waits for insects.

4   When something comes near her door, she can sense the motions above her nest. She pushes the lid open quickly. But the trap door is so strong that she could be locked out. So she leaves her hind legs and a part of her body under the open lid. Then the spider grabs the surprised insect in her jaws. Down they go into her nest! The trap-door spider does not need a web.

1. A spider that does not build a web to catch its food is the
     a. garden spider.   c. trap-door spider.
     b. wolf spider.   d. lace spider.

2. The word in paragraph 2 that means *tiny green plants* is

    _____.

3. The words "a lid of dirt and webbing" in paragraph 1 refer to the

    _____.

4. The story does not say so, but it makes you think that the trap-door spider
     a. plants a small garden.
     b. eats other insects for food.
     c. leaves the nest at night.

5. The trap-door spider hunts
     a. after dark.   c. when the moon is out.
     b. during the day.   d. in the winter.

6. The trap door is so strong that it could lock the spider out.
     Yes   No   Does not say

7. On the whole, this story is about
     a. spiders that build webs.
     b. materials that spiders use to hunt.
     c. spiders that do not build webs.

8. What is meant by the sentence, "She is as sly as a fox"?
     a. The trap-door spider is tricky.
     b. The trap-door spider is playful.
     c. The trap-door spider is brown.

9. Which of these sentences do you think is right?
     a. The trap-door spider is afraid to leave its nest.
     b. The spider builds a nest to keep out other insects.
     c. The trap-door spider moves quickly when hunting.

Birds That "See" with Their Ears

1   Most birds live in places where it is light during the day. They can use their eyes to see where they are going. The oilbirds of South America live in dark caves. They use their ears to help them find their way.

2   The oilbird is a brown bird with owl-like eyes. It nests on a high ledge in an ink-black cave. It only leaves the cave at night to hunt for food and returns before dawn.

3   The oilbird flies in circles in its dark cave. There is not enough light for it to see clearly with its large eyes. As the oilbird flies, it uses its voice to make sharp, clicking sounds. These clicks bounce off the cave walls and become echoes.

4   The oilbird listens to the echoes it has made. If the echoes take a long time to come back, the bird knows it is far from the wall. If they return quickly, the bird is close to it. In this way, the oilbird hears how far it is from the wall.

5   Oilbirds spend their lives in the dark, yet they never bump into the walls of their cave homes. We say that oilbirds "see" with their ears.

1. Oilbirds live
   - a. on mountain tops.
   - c. on the ground.
   - b. in dark caves.
   - d. in nests in trees.

2. The word in paragraph 2 that means *a shelf* or *a ridge of rock* is

   _____.

3. The words "owl-like" in paragraph 2 describe the oilbird's

   _____.

4. The story does not say so, but it makes you think that
   - a. oilbirds do not like light.
   - b. oilbirds are blind.
   - c. most birds sing only in the dark.

5. Oilbirds leave their caves at night to
   - a. exercise.
   - c. hunt for food.
   - b. play.
   - d. see their friends.

6. Oilbirds make clicking sounds that become echoes.
   Yes   No   Does not say

7. On the whole, this story is about
   - a. echoes that are heard in caves.
   - b. owls that live in the dark.
   - c. the oilbirds of South America.

8. How do the clicking sounds help an oilbird inside a cave? (Check the story again.)
   - a. They are signals to other birds.
   - b. They become echoes that help it find its way.
   - c. They mean the bird is getting ready to eat.

9. Which of these sentences do you think is right?
   - a. Oilbirds have good hearing.
   - b. Oilbirds live near oil wells.
   - c. Oilbirds often bump into the cave walls.

Two Ways of Doing Business

1   People sometimes change their way of doing business. In a certain village in Africa, people are using money for the first time. They are doing business with the modern world.

2   Before this tribe used money, families exchanged goods. People came to the market in the village to trade. At the market, people traded things they had for things they needed. A family exchanged bowls they had made for food to eat. Now people must use money to buy what they want.

3   Before using money, people helped one another. The father, who was head of the family, gave food and clothing to his sons and their families. In return, the sons worked for their father. Now people no longer work for one another free. Instead, they are paid for the work they do.

4   When a new road was needed, everyone in the village helped build it. Now people must pay money to the village chief for roads and schools. The chief hires workers to build these new projects. More and better roads and schools are being built.

5   It is not easy for people to change a way of doing business.

To change from trading goods to using money and paying taxes takes time.

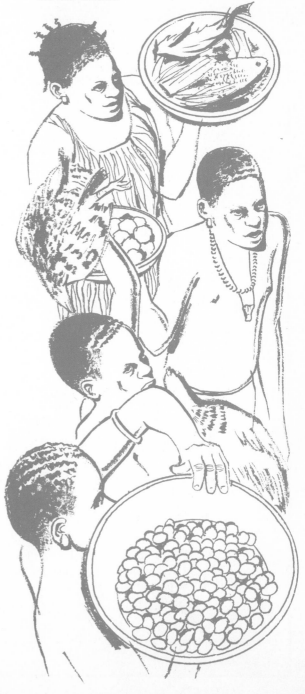

1. The people in a certain village in Africa are now
   - a. trading goods at the market.
   - b. using money.
   - c. making everything they need.
   - d. working free.

2. The word in paragraph 2 that means *traded* is

   _____ .

3. The words "head of the family" in paragraph 3 refer to the word

   _____ .

4. The story does not say so, but it makes you think that
   - a. Africans do not change their ways of doing business.
   - b. families do not help one another in the same ways now.
   - c. Africans do not use money.

5. Before the people of this African village used money,
   - a. there was no market.
   - b. there were no roads.
   - c. they could not do business.
   - d. they traded things.

6. Now the people pay taxes for building roads and schools.
   Yes   No   Does not say

7. On the whole, this story is about
   - a. changing from trading goods to using money.
   - b. exchanging goods for schools.
   - c. building roads across Africa.

8. Why did these people start using money? (Check the story again.)
   - a. They ran out of things to trade.
   - b. They wanted to do business as it was done in other places.
   - c. They didn't have any way to pay their taxes.

9. Which of these sentences do you think is right?
   - a. Trading goods is an older way of doing business.
   - b. Using money has made families work together.
   - c. It is easy for people to change their ways of doing things.

Business Between Countries

1   People within a country do business together. They buy goods, or products, from one another and sell products to others.

2   Different countries do business together, too. One country may buy and bring in things from another country. This is called importing products. The same country may also sell and send things to another country. This is called exporting products.

3   The Netherlands is a small country better known to us as Holland. It lies in the low country of Europe on the North Sea.

4   Holland has a steel-making industry which needs iron. This ore is found in some parts of the world, but Holland has none. The little country must import it. Ships carry the ore to the Netherlands from places like Canada and Africa.

5   Holland grows millions of flower bulbs every year. The country is famous for the beautiful tulips grown from these bulbs. Large numbers of tulip bulbs are dug up, dried, and exported to many countries.

6   Do you have tulips growing in your garden? Perhaps they are growing from bulbs brought from Holland.

FIND THE ANSWERS

1. Holland is a small country on the
   - a. Pacific Ocean.
   - b. North Sea.
   - c. Atlantic Ocean.
   - d. Mediterranean Sea.

2. The words "sell and send things to another country" in paragraph 2 explain the word _____.

3. The words "this ore" in paragraph 4 refer to the word

   _____.

4. The story does not say so, but it makes you think that
   - a. Holland is much smaller than the United States.
   - b. Holland is one of the largest countries in Asia.
   - c. Holland does not have any industry.

5. Every year Holland grows millions of
   - a. trees.
   - b. vegetables.
   - c. grains.
   - d. flower bulbs.

6. Holland imports iron ore from the United States.
   Yes   No   Does not say

7. On the whole, this story is about
   - a. tulips.
   - b. importing and exporting.
   - c. the low countries in Europe.

8. Why does Holland import some things? (Check the story again.)
   - a. The people there like to trade things.
   - b. Holland needs some things from other countries.
   - c. There are not enough people in Holland who like tulips.

9. Which of these sentences do you think is right?
   - a. Holland depends on other countries to keep its industry going.
   - b. Holland does not trade with other countries.
   - c. Holland is a large country with many natural resources.

Animals Mean Wealth

1 Different things are important in different communities. What a community thinks is important can change the way it carries on its business.

2 The Navaho (nav′ ə hō) Indians live on large reservations in Arizona, New Mexico, and Utah. They raise sheep and horses as a business. The animals feed on grass growing on Navaho land.

3 The Indians got sheep and horses from the Spaniards in the 1600s. Later, the sheep and horses became important to the Navahos for wool, meat, and travel. But the animals were also a sign of wealth. A family with many sheep or horses was important in the community.

4 At one time, the Navahos had more than a million animals. But the sheep were eating the grass down to the ground. Each horse ate more grass than five sheep. Even the roots of the grass were dying, and the ground was beginning to wash away in the rain. There were too many animals. Without grass to eat, the animals would die. The Navahos themselves would not have enough food.

5 The government wanted to help. It asked the Navahos to make their herds smaller. It was a sad time for the people. Large herds were very important to them.

1. The Navaho Indians live in
    a. Mexico.   c. Arizona.
    b. California.   d. Colorado.

2. The word in paragraph 2 that means *places where Indians live* is

    _____ .

3. The words "were eating the grass down to the ground" in paragraph 4

    tell about the word _____ .

4. The story does not say so, but it makes you think that
    a. the Navahos need more animals.
    b. too many animals can kill the grass.
    c. the Navahos grow many crops.

5. The Navaho Indians raise
    a. pigs and chickens.   c. cows and goats.
    b. corn and wheat.   d. sheep and horses.

6. The Navahos raise sheep just for food.
    Yes   No   Does not say

7. On the whole, this story is about
    a. the government in Mexico.
    b. the Navahos and their animals.
    c. Indian reservations.

8. Why did the Navahos want to keep large herds of animals? (Check the
    story again.)
    a. Large herds were important to the Navahos.
    b. The Navahos eat a lot.
    c. The Navahos need the hides of the animals for clothing.

9. Which of these sentences do you think is right?
    a. The Navahos were running out of food for their animals.
    b. The Navahos did not have enough animals.
    c. The Navahos liked small herds of animals.

A Changing Language

1 The English language is different from any other language. Yet English words do not stay the same. Our language is always changing. We need new words for new inventions and new ideas. Different words come into use, or older words are used in a new way.

2 English can change by borrowing words from other languages. *Tomato* was borrowed from Mexico and *pajamas* from India. The word *coffee* came from Turkey, and *tea* came from China. Now new space and science words are being borrowed from other countries, too.

3 New words are also made by adding two words together. *Straw-*

berry, popcorn, and *grandfather* are words made up of two parts.

4 Sometimes new words are shorter forms of older words. The word *photo* was made from *photograph* by cutting off the end of the longer word. *Plane* was made by cutting off the front part of *airplane. Smog* was made by using only the first two and last two letters from the words *smoke* and *fog.*

5 The names of people and products can become new words. Our *sandwich* was named after a man named Sandwich. Scotch Tape, Band-Aid, and Jello were names made up by the companies that first made the products.

1. The English language needs new words for new
   - a. books and magazines.
   - c. inventions and ideas.
   - b. movies and TV plays.
   - d. stories and fairy tales.

2. The word in paragraph 2 that means *taking* or *using as one's own* is

   _____.

3. The words "always changing" in paragraph 1 refer to our

   _____.

4. The story does not say so, but it makes you think that
   - a. all new words are borrowed.
   - b. languages do not stay the same.
   - c. all new words come from company names.

5. Scotch tape was named by
   - a. a Scotchman.
   - c. a child.
   - b. a country.
   - d. a company.

6. Other languages borrow words from English.
   Yes   No   Does not say

7. On the whole, this story is about
   - a. borrowing other languages.
   - b. the English language.
   - c. naming new products.

8. Why is the English language always changing? (Check the story again.)
   - a. People get tired of using the same words.
   - b. We need new words for new inventions and ideas.
   - c. English must become more like French and German.

9. Which of these sentences do you think is right?
   - a. New words come about in different ways.
   - b. There are no new words in our language.
   - c. People in space talk a different language.

chat

cat

faße

Thousands of Sounds

1   Most people in our country speak English. In some lands, people speak other languages. There are over 2,000 languages spoken throughout the world.

2   You probably know that every language has its own words, or vocabulary. If you want to learn a foreign language, you must learn its vocabulary. For example, our word "cat" is *chat* (shä) in French and *Katze* (kät′ zə) in German.

3   You must learn what the words mean, and you must say them in the right way. Words are made up of sounds, and different languages have different sounds. There are thousands of language sounds. When you speak English, you are using only about fifty of them.

4   Have you ever heard a foreign language spoken on television? Did it sound as if it was spoken very fast? Maybe it was. Some languages are spoken faster than others. English is spoken more slowly than French. French people speak about 350 syllables per minute. Using English, we speak 220. But some South Seas peoples speak only fifty syllables per minute.

5   Women speak faster than men. In America, women speak about 175 words per minute, but men speak only 150. How many words per minute do you speak?

FIND THE ANSWERS

1. The main language spoken in the United States is
   - a. French.
   - b. German.
   - c. foreign.
   - d. English.

2. The word in paragraph 2 that means *something from another country* is _____.

3. The words "speak faster than men" in paragraph 5 refer to the word _____.

4. The story does not say so, but it makes you think that
   - a. learning another language takes time.
   - b. all languages use the same sounds.
   - c. most people in the world speak English.

5. Words are made up of
   - a. language.
   - b. English.
   - c. sounds.
   - d. pictures.

6. There is a word for "cat" in French.
   Yes   No   Does not say

7. On the whole, this story is about
   - a. how fast people talk.
   - b. traveling in foreign countries.
   - c. the many sounds of many languages.

8. What must you do if you want to learn a foreign language? (Check the story again.)
   - a. You must learn its vocabulary.
   - b. You must live in the foreign country.
   - c. You must learn to speak French first.

9. Which of these sentences do you think is right?
   - a. Men speak faster than women.
   - b. All foreign languages are spoken faster than English.
   - c. English is only one of many languages.

English Can Be Strange

1   Have you ever heard someone speak in a language that you couldn't understand? Perhaps it was French. But it could have been English!

2   At times, English can sound as different as another language. It is spoken by one out of ten people in the world. Yet there are many differences between the "Queen's English" and American English.

3   In England, the Queen's English is the way radio and TV announcers say words. It is thought to be the most correct way to pronounce words. When the doctor asks you to say "ah," you are using the sound that the English use in the words *bath* and *dance*.

4   Words can have different meanings, too. English children go to a "sweets shop." American children would visit a candy store. They watch the "telly." Americans watch TV. The English go to "flicks," while we go to movies.

5   Railroad tracks are "metals." A freight car is a "goods wagon." They call the subway the "underground." A "flyover" is our overpass. They call an automobile hood a "bonnet." Our car trunk is a "boot" to them, and our horn is a "hooter."

6   If you went to England, could you understand the language?

1. In England, the "Queen's English" is spoken by all
   a. Americans.   c. people.
   b. announcers.   d. children.

2. The word in paragraph 3 that means *to speak* or *to say* is

   _____ .

3. The words "can sound as different as another language" in paragraph

   2 refer to the word _____ .

4. The story does not say so, but it makes you think that
   a. people watch television in both England and America.
   b. English children never eat candy.
   c. the same language always sounds the same.

5. The Americans call them movies, but the English call them
   a. metals.   b. sweets   c. goods wagons.   d. flicks.

6. English is spoken by three out of ten people in the world.
   Yes   No   Does not say

7. On the whole, this story is about
   a. going to see an English doctor.
   b. American and English television programs and movies.
   c. differences between American and English speech.

8. Why might an American have trouble understanding the English?
   (Check the story again.)
   a. Some of the words the English use are different.
   b. The English speak a foreign language.
   c. The people in England speak only to their Queen.

9. Which of these sentences do you think is right?
   a. The English do not have cars or television sets.
   b. The English and the Americans cannot understand one another.
   c. The "Queen's English" would be easier to understand than
      French.

Artists Who Didn't Draw People

1   Moslems (moz' ləmz) are people who believe in the teachings of a man called Mohammed. Mohammed lived in the 600s. One of the things he said was that no one should make copies of living things.

2   In the 600s and 700s, the Moslems took over the Middle East. The artists of the Middle East had to follow the laws of Mohammed. For many years, they could not copy living figures. They could not draw people.

3   Do you wonder what the Moslem artists did? They used their imaginations to make many beautiful and colorful designs. To make designs, they often used the shapes of flowers. Sometimes they used the curving lines of vines and palm leaves.

4   The Moslem artists used designs to decorate many different things. They decorated the walls of buildings and the pages of books. Decoration became the most important part of Moslem art.

5   After a while, some Moslem artists could paint pictures with people in them. In Persia in the 1400s, the artists made beautiful paintings for books. Even then, decoration still filled the pictures. The people in the pictures looked strange. They looked as if they were living in a dream world.

FIND THE ANSWERS

1. People who believe in the teachings of Mohammed are called
   a. artists.
   b. Americans.
   c. Moslems.
   d. Persians.

2. The word in paragraph 3 that means *forms* or *outlines* is

   _____.

3. The words "beautiful and colorful" in paragraph 3 refer to the word

   _____.

4. The story does not say so, but it makes you think that
   a. artists of the Middle East could not paint.
   b. Moslem artists drew pictures using only straight lines.
   c. Moslem artists used curving lines to make designs.

5. For many years, Moslem artists could not draw
   a. figures.
   b. lines.
   c. buildings.
   d. mountains.

6. Decoration became the most important part of Moslem art.
   Yes   No   Does not say

7. On the whole, this story is about
   a. Moslem artists.   b. Persia.   c. a dream world.

8. What is meant by the sentence, "The people looked as if they were living in a dream world"?
   a. The people did not seem to be real.
   b. The people were dreaming about another world.
   c. The people were asleep.

9. Which of these sentences do you think is right?
   a. Art in the Middle East changed after the Moslems took over.
   b. The artists of the Middle East would not obey the Moslems.
   c. Moslem artists painted with palm leaves.

Paintings from the Earth

1   Have you ever used watercolors to make a picture? Have you made designs with finger paints? Many pictures are made by putting colored paint on paper or cloth. Pictures painted in this way will last a long time.

2   The Navaho (nav′ ə hō) Indians in the Southwest make paintings that last less than one day. These designs are called sand paintings. They are different from all other paintings.

3   Using bits of powdered and colored rock, the Navahos "paint" on a large cowhide or on smooth sand. Sand flows through their fingers to make paintings. The designs are often of their Indian gods. They also use pieces of flowers or meal and other vegetable materials.

4   Once, sand paintings were made only by a medicine man when someone was ill. The medicine man hoped the Navaho gods would like his design and make the sick well.

5   Today, most sand paintings are made for special Indian ceremonies. These beautiful paintings are always destroyed before the sun sets. They are not painted for people to enjoy. They are painted to please the Navaho gods.

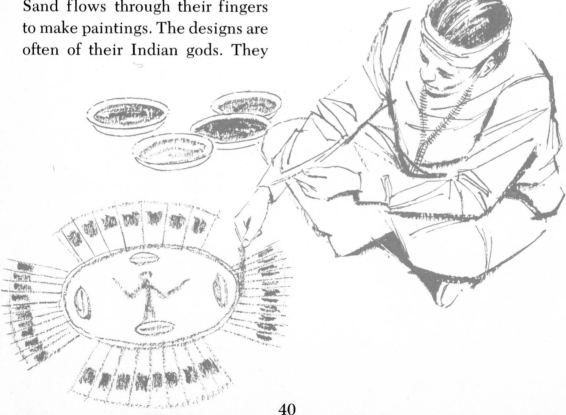

1. The Navaho Indians make paintings that last
   a. one week.
   b. less than a year.
   c. less than a day.
   d. a long time.

2. The word in paragraph 5 that means *torn apart* or *ruined* is

   _____.

3. The words "The designs are often of their Indian gods" in paragraph

   3 refer to _____ _____.

4. The story does not say so, but it makes you think that sand paintings
   a. are done to make money.
   b. are made every day.
   c. are not meant to last.

5. Sand paintings are made of
   a. powdered rock.
   b. finger paints.
   c. sand from the beach.
   d. oil paints.

6. Sand paintings are made for the Navahos to enjoy.
   Yes   No   Does not say

7. On the whole, this story is about
   a. Indian sand paintings.
   b. the Southwest.
   c. beautiful sunsets.

8. Why do the Navahos make sand paintings? (Check the story again.)
   a. They want to show they are fine artists.
   b. They want to please their Indian gods.
   c. They want to help the medicine man.

9. Which of these sentences do you think is right?
   a. Sand paintings make people ill.
   b. Sand paintings are made for people to enjoy.
   c. Sand paintings have special meanings for the Navahos.

They Carved Totem Poles

1   The Haida (hī′ də) Indians live in Alaska and Northwest Canada. The Haida are well known for their wood carvings. Most people know about their carvings of animals and people on tall poles. These decorated posts are called totem poles.

2   The Haida carved on wood long before other peoples came to their land. They carved designs on their canoes and on wooden boxes. They decorated everything they made.

3   The designs told stories and were thought to bring good luck. For carving, the Haida used sharp stones, pieces of bone, and shells. Think how hard it must have been to carve wood with a stone tool!

4   Later, the Haida got metal tools from visitors. These metal tools made carving easier.

5   In the 1800s, the Haida carved many totem poles. They used logs from cedar trees. The first totem poles had only one carved figure. Later, totem poles had many figures, one above the other. The figures were of people, birds, fish, and other animals. The poles were 40 to 70 feet high. There were many totem poles in a Haida village.

6   The Haida today carve objects to sell to visitors. The totem poles they once carved are looked upon as works of art.

1. The Haida are well known for their carvings made of
   a. ivory.   c. soap.
   b. wood.   d. bone.

2. The word in paragraph 2 that means *made designs on* or *made beautiful*

   is _____ .

3. The words "one above the other" in paragraph 5 refer to the word

   _____ .

4. The story does not say so, but it makes you think that the Haida
   a. took a long time to carve with stone tools.
   b. carved designs on the doors of every house.
   c. carved designs on the trees in the forests.

5. The Haida once carved with
   a. wooden poles.   c. pieces of bone.
   b. axes.   d. their teeth.

6. Today, the Haida show visitors how they do their carving.
   Yes   No   Does not say

7. On the whole, this story is about
   a. how to carve.   b. cedar logs.   c. Haida carvings.

8. Why did the Haida carve designs on everything they made? (Check
   the story again.)
   a. They thought their carvings would bring good luck.
   b. They liked to work with stone tools.
   c. They made decorated canoes to sell to neighbors.

9. Which of these sentences do you think is right?
   a. The Haida carve for fun.
   b. Some Haida totem poles are very old.
   c. The Haida learned to carve from other people.

A Stone Age People

1   Many centuries ago, all people had to gather seeds and plants to eat. They did not know how to farm or raise animals for food. Because they used stone tools and weapons, we call them the Stone Age people.

2   There are people who still live much like these Stone Age people lived. They live in places that are hard to reach. Because they have met few outsiders, they do not know about modern inventions. They have not traded ways of doing things with others.

3   For 25,000 years, groups of peoples have lived alone in the middle of Australia. One of these groups is the Arunta (ə rən′ tə) tribe. They do not know how to farm, nor do they raise sheep or cattle.

4   The Aruntas spend most of their time searching for food and water. The men hunt animals with stone-tipped spears. The women and children look for roots, seeds, and nuts. They use sticks to dig up the roots. Several Arunta families live together. They have no houses. At night, they sleep around small fires.

5   Now other peoples are moving into the center of Australia. In time, the Aruntas will no longer be a Stone Age people.

1. Many centuries ago, people got food by
    a. going to the store.   c. gathering plants and seeds.
    b. raising animals.   d. growing crops on farms.

2. The word in paragraph 4 that means *looking for* is

   _____.

3. The words "they sleep around small fires" in paragraph 4 refer to the

   _____.

4. The story does not say so, but it makes you think that
    a. people in Australia live in different ways.
    b. the Aruntas do not like to hunt.
    c. everyone in Australia lives in large cities.

5. The Arunta women and children dig with
    a. sticks.   c. shovels.
    b. stones.   d. their hands.

6. Each Arunta family lives by itself.
    Yes   No   Does not say

7. On the whole, this story is about
    a. stone-tipped spears.
    b. the Arunta tribe.
    c. trading ways of doing things.

8. Why do the Aruntas still live the way they do? (Check the story again.)
    a. They have not yet learned new ways from other peoples.
    b. They do not want to change their way of living.
    c. Other people are moving in and living with the Aruntas.

9. Which of these sentences do you think is right?
    a. Not all groups of peoples in the world today live alike.
    b. The Aruntas live near the big cities in the middle of Australia.
    c. The Aruntas live in modern homes.

The Mayor Wore a Turban

1   Many cities in the world have a mayor, who is head of the city government. Doña Felisa Rincón del Guatier was a strong mayor of San Juan, the capital city of Puerto Rico. To the people of San Juan, Doña Fela was not only a mayor but also a warm friend.

2   Like other mayors, Doña Fela wanted good things for her city. Puerto Ricans like to play baseball. Doña Fela saw that they got a large stadium. Many of the poor people in San Juan needed help when they got sick. Doña Fela's favorite work was the building of a new medical center.

3   Unlike other mayors, Doña Fela usually wore a turban and often carried a fan. She held parties for old women. She gave candy and toys to children. When a poor man had a hole in his roof, he went to see Doña Fela. She helped him get materials to build a new roof.

4   The weather in San Juan is always warm, and many children there never see snow. One winter, Doña Fela had a plane full of snow flown to San Juan for the children to enjoy.

5   Doña Fela took care of big problems in her city, but she also remembered the little ones.

1. San Juan is a
   a. country.   c. city.
   b. river.   d. state.

2. The word in paragraph 2 that means *a large building where games are played* is _____.

3. The words "who is head of the city government" in paragraph 1 refer to

   _____.

4. The story does not say so, but it makes you think that
   a. Doña Fela liked children.
   b. Doña Fela liked candy.
   c. Doña Fela liked big hats.

5. Puerto Ricans liked to play
   a. baseball.   c. football.
   b. soccer.   d. basketball.

6. Doña Fela wanted bad things for her city.
   Yes   No   Does not say

7. On the whole, the story is about
   a. a senator   b. a president.   c. a mayor.

8. Why was a new medical center built in San Juan? (Check the story.)
   a. Doctors like to work in new buildings.
   b. Many poor people needed help when they got sick.
   c. There were not enough doctors in San Juan.

9. Which of these sentences do you think is right?
   a. San Juan is in the Pacific Ocean.
   b. It does not snow in San Juan.
   c. San Juan is a small city.

Space for a Hammock

1   Brazil is the largest country in South America. It is almost as big as the United States. Most of the country lies in the tropics, where it is warm and wet. And most of the center of Brazil has few people.

2   In the warm, wooded central part live Indian tribes who have no enemies or modern tools. They have no calendars, cities, or schools. Wild animals and birds live near their villages, but the Indians do not like to hunt them. Instead, they cook fish and a vegetable that looks something like a sweet potato.

3   The Indians' houses look like giant bowls turned upside down. Several families live in each house, which is made of poles and covered with plant fibers. Each family has a place for a cooking fire. Each person has space for a hammock. A wife's hammock is hung below her husband's. The children sleep in small hammocks near their parents. People in the village sleep twelve hours each night and take naps besides.

4   These Indians are protected by laws. No one can bother them or change the way in which they live. They can live in the same easy-going way for as long as they like.

1. In the center of Brazil there are
   a. large cities.
   b. no people.
   c. Indian tribes.
   d. many deserts.

2. The word in paragraph 4 that means *worry* or *disturb* is

   _____ .

3. The words "where it is warm and wet" in paragraph 1 refer to the

   _____ .

4. The story does not say so, but it makes you think that
   a. the way these Indians live may not change.
   b. this tribe does a lot of hard work.
   c. these Indians have their own hunting grounds.

5. Everyone sleeps in his own
   a. bed.
   b. hammock.
   c. cot.
   d. sleeping bag.

6. The houses look like giant bowls turned upside down.
   Yes   No   Does not say

7. On the whole, this story is about
   a. giant bowls in Brazil.
   b. cities in South America.
   c. Indians in Brazil.

8. Why are these people protected by laws? (Check the story again.)
   a. They do not know how to make their own laws.
   b. Other tribes might start a war with them.
   c. They have a right to keep their easygoing ways.

9. Which of these sentences do you think is right?
   a. Different peoples live in different ways.
   b. Each family in the village has its own house.
   c. The Indians of Brazil live in bowls.

The Puzzle of the Pyramids

1   When the Greeks reached Egypt long ago, they found many stone buildings. They named the buildings pyramids. The Greeks did not know how the people of Egypt had built these big pyramids. And we still do not know exactly how.

2   The people of Egypt believed in life after death. Egyptians put things a person might need in this after-life near the body. The bodies of rulers were placed inside the pyramids.

3   The Great Pyramid was built for King Cheops (kē′ ops). It was 482 feet high and covered more than 13 acres of land. It was made of 2,300,000 pieces of stone, each weighing about 5,000 pounds.

4   How did the people move such big stones? Perhaps they floated them down the river on rafts. They may have put the stones on rollers. People could have pulled the stones up sloping roads to the sides of the pyramids. The stones fit together so well that a knife cannot be pushed between them.

5   Century after century, winds blow yellow sand around the pyramids. Rulers have come and gone. Everything seems to change except the pyramids. They remain a 5,000-year-old puzzle.

1. The pyramids were named by
    a. the Greeks.   c. King Cheops.
    b. the Egyptians.   d. the Indians.

2. The word in paragraph 4 that means *slanting* or *tilting* is

   _____.

3. The words "made of 2,300,000 pieces of stone" in paragraph 3 describe

   the _____.

4. The story does not say so, but it makes you think that
    a. it was easy to build the pyramids.
    b. the pyramids were floated down the river.
    c. the people who built the pyramids were good builders.

5. The people in Egypt believed
    a. that blowing sand would be   c. in making wooden houses.
      good for the pyramids.   d. in burying their kings
    b. in life after death.   underground.

6. The pyramids were made of small stones that were easy to carry.
    Yes   No   Does not say

7. On the whole, this story is about
    a. moving heavy stones.
    b. building the pyramids.
    c. Egyptian kings.

8. Why did the Egyptians build the pyramids? (Check the story again.)
    a. The pyramids were built as tombs for their kings.
    b. They wanted everyone to work hard.
    c. This was their way of building a castle.

9. Which of these sentences do you think is right?
    a. The pyramids were built to make the desert more interesting.
    b. The pyramids were very well built.
    c. The pyramids had no use.

A Shortcut Between Two Oceans

1   In 1904, Americans began the hardest building task they had ever tried. They started to dig the Panama Canal.

As you know, our country lies between the Atlantic and the Pacific Oceans. There was no easy way for ships to go from ocean to ocean. They had to sail almost 8,000 miles around South America.

2   The country of Panama lies between North and South America. In one place, Panama is only 28 miles wide. Americans wanted to build a canal across this narrow piece of land.

3   Panama had high mountains and thick jungles. It also had mosquitoes which carried yellow fever and malaria. Men working there often became sick and died.

4   First, our country sent men to destroy as many mosquitoes and their eggs as they could. Then doctors used drugs to fight the diseases. At last, big earth-moving machines were sent to Panama, and hundreds of men began to build the Canal.

5   Work went slowly as thousands of tons of earth were moved. After ten years, the Panama Canal was finally opened. The first ship passed through the Canal in 1914. Today, ships from many lands use the Canal. It is a shortcut between two oceans.

1. The Americans began to build the Panama Canal in
   a. 1940.   c. 1914.
   b. 1904.   d. 1900.

2. The word in paragraph 1 that means *job* or *thing to be done* is

   _____ .

3. The words "carried yellow fever and malaria" in paragraph 3 refer to

   the word _____ .

4. The story does not say so, but it makes you think that the Panama Canal
   a. was easy to build.
   b. gave the workers no problems.
   c. helped speed up trade.

5. Before building the Canal, our country sent men to destroy many
   a. wild animals.   c. mosquitoes.
   b. snakes.   d. villages.

6. Panama is flat, desert country.
   Yes   No   Does not say

7. On the whole, this story is about
   a. building the Panama Canal.
   b. malaria and yellow fever.
   c. doctors and drugs.

8. The Panama Canal was built in order to
   a. divide Panama in half.
   b. make a shortcut between the Atlantic and Pacific Oceans.
   c. help doctors destroy the mosquitoes.

9. Which of these sentences do you think is right?
   a. The people of Panama asked America to build the Canal.
   b. The Panama Canal is hundreds of miles long.
   c. Panama lies between the Atlantic and Pacific Oceans.

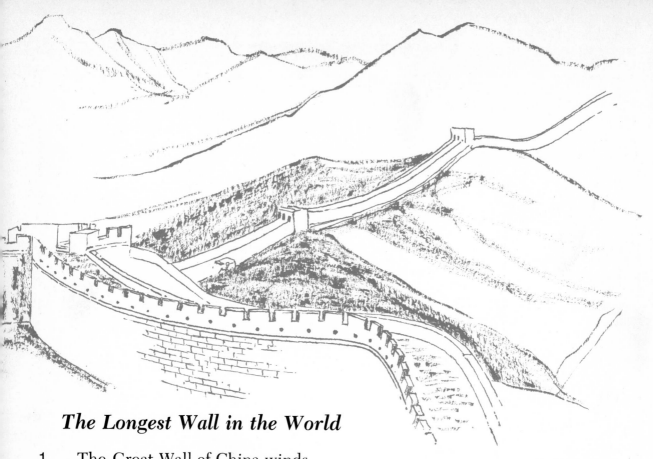

The Longest Wall in the World

1   The Great Wall of China winds across the country like a giant stone snake. It is 1,500 miles long.

2   The wall crosses mountains and rivers. It reaches from the ocean on the east to the desert on the west.

3   The Chinese began their wall more than 2,000 years ago. They worked on it for hundreds of years. The Chinese wanted to keep out their enemies.

4   At the bottom, the wall is 25 feet wide. At the top, it is about 15 feet wide. The sides of the wall are made of stone and brick, while the inside is filled with earth.

5   Parts of the wall rise as high as a three-story building. Placed 100 yards apart are tall towers. Lookouts could stand in the towers to watch for enemies approaching. The road on top of the wall is wide enough for two wagons to pass.

6   If we were to build such a wall now, we would use modern machines. But the Chinese had to build the wall by hand. If the wall were in our country, it would reach from the state of New York to Nebraska. The Great Wall of China is the longest wall ever built.

1. The Great Wall of China is
   a. 15,000 inches long.
   b. 150 feet long.
   c. 10,500 yards long.
   d. 1,500 miles long.

2. The word in paragraph 5 that means *coming near* or *coming up to* is

   _____.

3. The words "the longest wall ever built" in paragraph 6 refer to the

   _____ _____ _____ _____.

4. The story does not say so, but it makes you think that the Great Wall
   a. was hard to build.
   b. has a gate every 100 yards.
   c. is used as a road for cars today.

5. The inside of the Great Wall is filled with
   a. iron.
   b. earth.
   c. brick.
   d. stone.

6. The Great Wall of China was built by hand.
   Yes   No   Does not say

7. On the whole, this story is about
   a. tall towers.
   b. the Great Wall of China.
   c. Chinese lookouts.

8. What is meant by the sentence, "The Great Wall winds across the country like a giant stone snake"?
   a. It stops the wind from blowing.
   b. It can move.
   c. It has many curves.

9. Which of these sentences do you think is right?
   a. The Great Wall of China was built with modern machinery.
   b. The Great Wall was like a long fort.
   c. The Great Wall goes from New York to Nebraska.

Naming Children

1   Among most peoples in the world, children are given names. In the United States children have a family name, or a "last name," and a first name. Most also have a middle name. However, not all people name children in the same way.

2   Some peoples believe that the spirits of those who have died are reborn in babies. To name a baby, the parents begin by saying the names of the child's ancestors. The baby may sneeze, smile, or cry when a certain name is said. The parents think that means the ancestor is reborn in the baby. The baby is given that name.

3   Some peoples change their names. Navaho Indians change their names when they want new ones. The Navaho can decide to use the mother's last name rather than the father's. He or she may want an English name in place of an Indian one. The Navahos do not think it important to keep the same name.

4   In some parts of Africa, a baby's name is kept secret. No strangers are allowed to learn it. People there believe that the name is part of the child. They think that anyone who learns the name will have power over the child.

1. In the United States most children have
   a. a first name.   c. three names.
   b. only a last name.   d. a middle and a last name.

2. The word in paragraph 4 that means *kept from others* is

   _____.

3. The words "sneeze, smile, or cry" in paragraph 2 refer to the

   _____.

4. The story does not say so, but it makes you think that
   a. parents everywhere tell all their friends the name of their baby.
   b. peoples have different reasons for choosing a baby's name.
   c. all children are named after their ancestors.

5. In some parts of Africa, strangers are not told the name of
   a. a baby.   c. the ancestors.
   b. the family.   d. the mother.

6. Navaho Indians always change their names.
   Yes   No   Does not say

7. On the whole, this story is about
   a. giving ancestors a name.
   b. changing the name of an African child.
   c. how people are given their names.

8. Why is it easy for Navaho Indians to change their name? (Check the story.)
   a. They feel that it is not important to keep the same name.
   b. Whenever they sneeze, they change their names.
   c. They believe a name is part of them.

9. Which of these sentences do you think is right?
   a. Children's names are not important to many parents.
   b. The parents in each country have different customs.
   c. Babies' names are always kept secret.

They Don't Watch Clocks

1   In cities in the United States, there are clocks in most stores, factories, and other buildings. Radio announcers give the correct time during the day. People here think that it is important to know the time. Most Americans have watches. They want to do certain things at certain times. They don't want to be late.

2   Time is not so important to peoples everywhere. Suppose you visit a country in South America. You would find that people living there do not like to rush. If you had an appointment with some friends, they would probably be late. They would not want to arrive on time.

3   In South America, even the radio programs may not begin right on time. Nor do the radio people think it important to announce the exact time.

4   In South America, many people think of a clock as a machine. They feel that people who do everything on time are letting clocks run their lives. They don't want a clock or any machine to have that much power over their lives.

1. There are clocks in most stores and factories in
   a. South America.   c. India.
   b. the United States.   d. South Africa.

2. The word in paragraph 3 that means *to tell* or *to let it be known* is

   _____.

3. The words "is not so important to peoples everywhere" in paragraph 2

   tell about the word _____.

4. The story does not say so, but it makes you think that
   a. people in South America are in a hurry.
   b. people in South America do not make appointments.
   c. there are fewer clocks in South America than in America.

5. The people of South America think of the clock as a
   a. machine.   c. friend.
   b. radio.   d. person.

6. Radio programs always begin on time in South America.
   Yes   No   Does not say

7. On the whole, this story is about
   a. factories in the United States.
   b. radio announcers in South America.
   c. peoples' feelings about time.

8. Why isn't time too important to the people of South America? (Check the story again.)
   a. It is too hot there to hurry to appointments.
   b. They don't want a machine to run their lives.
   c. They don't know how to tell time.

9. Which of these sentences do you think is right?
   a. Time means different things to different peoples.
   b. In the United States, it is a good idea to be late.
   c. Time is more important in South America than in America.

Hall of Apricot Forests

1   Would you like to buy bread from a store that was called *Garden of the Golden Valley*? Could you find a box of bandages in a shop called *Hall of Apricot Forests*?

2   When the Chinese people first came to the United States and opened stores, each store had a different name. The names made even ordinary places such as grocery stores and drugstores sound interesting.

3   Although the Chinese were eager to learn about the United States, they also wished their children to know and remember things from China. Even today, some Chinese American children go to school for a few hours at night to learn the history, writing, and languages of China.

4   Many of these students study hard and become good scientists and engineers. One fine Chinese American scientist is Chien-Shiung Wu. She makes careful experiments in physics. These experiments help to prove whether certain new ideas are right or wrong.

5   Chien-Shiung Wu was born in China and went to school there. Then she came to the United States and studied more. She became a U.S. citizen.

6   During World War II, Chien-Shiung experimented with nuclear material. Later, she made an important discovery. She showed scientists that there are always new ways to look at nature.

1. Chinese people have interesting names for their
    a. rivers.   c. stores.
    b. children.   d. cities.

2. The word in paragraph 2 that means *regular* or *usual* is

    _____.

3. The word "they" in paragraph 3 refers to the _____.

4. The story does not say so, but it makes you think that
    a. Chinese Americans eat a lot of bread.
    b. Chinese Americans are proud of both their countries.
    c. Chinese Americans do not like stores.

5. Chien-Shiung Wu made experiments in
    a. arithmetic.   c. algebra.
    b. physics.   d. spelling.

6. Many Chinese Americans have become good scientists.
    Yes   No   Does not say

7. On the whole, this story is about
    a. Indians.
    b. Chinese Americans.
    c. South Americans.

8. Why does Chien-Shiung Wu make careful experiments? (Check the story.)
    a. To prove whether certain ideas are right or wrong.
    b. To show us how to read physics books.
    c. To tell us about China.

9. Which of these sentences do you think is right?
    a. Chinese do not go to school.
    b. Scientists make new discoveries.
    c. World War II lasted two years.

Medea
(A Tale from Greek Mythology)

Medea was a beautiful princess who lived in the land of Colchis near the Black Sea. She was the granddaughter of the Sun, and so she had many magic powers.

Medea's father, Aeëtes, was the King of Colchis. He kept careful watch over his favorite treasure, the Golden Fleece. This was the golden wool of a sacred ram. The Golden Fleece hung from a tree in a dark forest in Colchis. A fierce dragon guarded the Fleece. No one had been able to touch the Golden Fleece because the dragon never went to sleep.

Then one day, a young man, Jason, came to Colchis in search of the Golden Fleece. Jason and his men came in a ship, the *Argos*, and they

were called *Argonauts*. If Jason could bring the Golden Fleece home, he would become king of his country.

Medea fell in love with Jason at once and wanted to help him. But her father was very angry that these strangers should land in Colchis. Jason said he would do anything the king wanted if he would give him the Golden Fleece. The king did not want to lose the Golden Fleece, so he decided to trick Jason.

"Very well," said Aeëtes. "Tomorrow, between sunrise and sunset, you must harness my fire-breathing bulls. You must plow a field and sow it with dragons' teeth. If you succeed, you may have the Golden Fleece. If you fail, I will cut out your tongue."

Aeëtes knew that no man could stand the terrible heat that blew from the noses of the bulls.

Medea understood what her father was trying to do, but she was not going to let anything happen to Jason. Late that night, she went to a dark cave. Carefully she mixed a magic ointment and gave it to Jason.

"Use this ointment tomorrow," said Medea. "For one day, neither fire nor iron can harm you."

Jason was very grateful. He promised to take Medea home with him and make her his queen.

Early the next morning, Jason went straight to the field. Because of Medea's ointment, he was able to harness the bulls and plow the field. Then he scattered the dragon's teeth. At once a crop of warriors sprang up. Jason threw a rock in the middle of them and they began to fight among themselves. By dark, all the warriors were dead.

Jason had done what the king asked, but Aeëtes still would not give up the Golden Fleece. Secretly, he decided to kill Jason and his men at dawn. When Medea learned this, she went straight to Jason.

"You have earned the Golden Fleece, but my father will never give it to you," said Medea. "You must take the Fleece and sail away before dawn. I will help you."

Medea led Jason into the forest where the shining Golden Fleece hung. The dragon guarding the Fleece roared, but Medea was not afraid. She cast a magic spell on the dragon and it fell asleep.

Quickly Jason reached up and took the Golden Fleece from the tree branch. He and Medea ran to the *Argos*. They woke the *Argonauts* and sailed safely away.

After many adventures, Jason and Medea brought the Golden Fleece home to Jason's land. But it gave them no real happiness. More and more, Medea began to use her magic powers to do evil things. At last, she got in a chariot drawn by two dragons. Medea rode off into a dark cloud and was never seen again. The Golden Fleece was hung in a Delphi temple.

602 words

64

II

Different Communities Need and Use Different Ways to Reach the Same Goals

In this section you will read about how different communities need and use different ways to reach the same goals. You will read about these things from the standpoint of history, biology, economics, sociology, art, geography, engineering, and anthropology.

Keep these questions in mind when you are reading.

1. Do all people approach a problem in the same way?

2. What are some problems that are common to all people?

3. What are some different ways that these problems are met?

4. Do other people's solutions to problems benefit us?

5. What are some things that cause people to use different ways to reach the same goals?

The King Is Also a Chief

1   In Africa, many of the people belong to tribes. The members of a tribe have much in common. They have the same ways of doing things, the same language, and the same forefathers. A tribe may have hundreds of thousands of members. Nevertheless, it is like a large family.

2   The leader of a tribe is the chief. The chief is the most important man in the tribe, and he is very powerful.

3   In Swaziland (swä′ zē land) in southern Africa, most of the people belong to the same tribe. The King of Swaziland is Sobhuza II (Sôb hü′ zä). King Sobhuza is also the chief of his tribe.

4   As chief, the King acts as rainmaker for the tribe. Once he took his rainmaking things when he visited another country. While he was there, it rained. The people of Swaziland were very proud of their chief's rainmaking powers.

5   The King and his mother take part in many colorful ceremonies. These ceremonies are part of the tribal way of life.

6   Once every year, there is a ceremony called First Fruit. It is supposed to make the King strong and powerful. There is much dancing, and thousands of people come to this happy event.

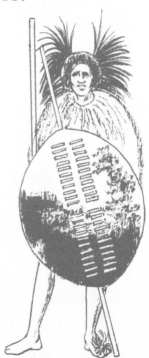

1. The members of a tribe have the same
   - a. language.
   - b. kind of car.
   - c. father.
   - d. house.

2. The word in paragraph 1 that means *even so* is

   _____.

3. The words "the most important man in the tribe" in paragraph 2 refer

   to the _____.

4. The story does not say so, but it makes you think that
   - a. King Sobhuza is chief of the American Indians.
   - b. many chiefs are rainmakers.
   - c. the medicine man is also the rainmaker.

5. The King of Swaziland
   - a. does not like ceremonies.
   - b. has little power.
   - c. stays in his village.
   - d. is a rainmaker.

6. In Africa, most of the people belong to the same tribe.
   Yes   No   Does not say

7. On the whole, this story is about
   - a. a tribe and their chief.
   - b. growing fruit.
   - c. happy events.

8. What is the ceremony called First Fruit supposed to do? (Check the story again.)
   - a. Make the fruit grow that year.
   - b. Help the chief get fruit from nearby tribes.
   - c. Make the King strong and powerful.

9. Which of these sentences do you think is right?
   - a. A chief and a king can sometimes mean the same thing.
   - b. The chief is no longer important in the life of the tribe.
   - c. It is always raining in Swaziland.

Island Lawyer

1   Hawaii is a string of more than twenty beautiful islands in the Pacific Ocean. In 1959, eight of the largest islands in the group became the fiftieth state in the United States.

2   In 1964, Hawaiians sent one of their best government leaders to speak for them in the United States Congress. She was Patsy Takemoto Mink, Congresswoman-at-Large.

3   As a child, Patsy Mink was very interested in "living things." Her family doctor, who took care of people, was her hero. In 1953, Patsy Mink became a lawyer, and she too began to take care of people.

4   Her job was to see that people were treated fairly. Patsy Mink was soon elected to the Hawaiian Congress and then to the Senate. Soon after that, she went to the United States Congress.

5   When Patsy Mink got to Washington, she worked hard to get new schools built. She got help for people coming home after wars.

6   Other Congresswomen have also written good laws to help people. Among these are Margaret Chase Smith from Maine, Florence P. Dwyer from New Jersey, and Edith S. Green from Oregon.

1. Hawaii became a state in
    a. 1914.
    c. 1900.
    b. 1959.
    d. 1859.

2. The word in paragraph 3 that means a *person known for doing great deeds* is _____.

3. The words "a string of beautiful islands" in paragraph 1 refer to _____.

4. The story does not say so, but it makes you think that
    a. Patsy Mink thought the country needed new schools.
    b. Hawaiians have many doctors.
    c. there are forty states in the United States.

5. Patsy Mink became a
    a. doctor.
    c. lawyer.
    b. teacher.
    d. artist.

6. The people of Hawaii elect a Congresswoman every year.
    Yes   No   Does not say

7. On the whole, this story is about
    a. the Hawaiian islands.
    b. doctors and lawyers.
    c. Congresswoman Patsy Mink.

8. Why did Hawaiians send Patsy Mink to Congress? (Check the story.)
    a. She knew all about Hawaii.
    b. She was one of their best government leaders.
    c. She liked to build schools.

9. Which of these sentences do you think is right?
    a. Hawaii is represented in the U. S. Congress.
    b. Hawaii is a small island surrounded by water.
    c. Hawaii has many rivers.

A Busy Woman

1   In the United States, laws to protect and help the people of the country are made by Congress. If each one of us who wanted a new law went to the Capitol, there would be too many people and too many ideas.

2   So people from each state vote for members of Congress, who go to Washington, D. C. These people will see that the ideas of the voters in their states are heard in Congress.

3   One member of Congress who makes good laws for her state is Barbara Jordan, Congresswoman from Texas. Jordan often meets with other members of Congress from Texas. Together, they decide what is best for their state.

Then she lets the rest of Congress know about the new laws she wants. She must get others to vote for these laws.

4   Jordan is a very good speaker. Other people in Congress listen to her. Almost half of the laws she has wanted have been passed.

5   Jordan also listens carefully to ideas for other states. If she thinks something will make a good law for the whole country, she will vote for it.

6   Jordan works on special government committees, too. She learns facts about special problems and tells the rest of Congress about them.

7   Barbara Jordan is one of the very busy people in Washington, D. C.

1. In the United States, laws are made by
   a. lawyers.
   c. Texas.
   b. Congress.
   d. presidents.

2. The word in paragraph 1 that means *to keep from harm* is

   _____.

3. The words "who makes good laws for her state" in paragraph 3 refer to

   _____.

4. The story does not say so, but it makes you think that
   a. Congress meets in Washington, D.C.
   b. women are not allowed in Congress.
   c. nobody speaks in Congress.

5. Barbara Jordan is from
   a. California.
   c. Alaska.
   b. Iowa.
   d. Texas.

6. People from Congress never go home.
   Yes   No   Does not say

7. On the whole, this is an article about
   a. a Texas Congresswoman.
   b. Texas history
   c. members of Congress.

8. How does Barbara Jordan decide what is best for Texans? (Check the story.)
   a. She meets with other Texans in Congress.
   b. She reads about Texas in history books.
   c. She asks everyone she meets.

9. Which of these sentences do you think is right?
   a. Congress does not pass laws.
   b. Congress passes ten laws a year.
   c. Barbara Jordan has helped many laws to pass.

Who Takes Care of the Young?

1   Who takes care of young animals until they are old enough to care for themselves? Different animals have different ways to care for their young.

2   The female bear feeds, protects, and teaches her cubs for over a year. Male bears do not like cubs and have been known to kill them. So the mother must keep the cubs away from their father.

3   Among some living things, it is the father who is in charge of the young. The male stickleback fish builds a nest in water weeds. As soon as the female has laid her eggs in the nest, she leaves.

4   The male stickleback guards the eggs. After the eggs hatch, the male watches over the young fish. If they go too far from the nest, their father carries them back in his mouth.

5   Wolves live together as a family. Both parents help raise the young. Both bring food to the pups and show them how to hunt. Both father and mother fight to protect their young against bears or other enemies.

1. The female bear
   a. leaves her cubs alone.   c. doesn't like cubs.
   b. gives her cubs away.   d. protects her cubs.

2. The word in paragraph 2 that means *guards from danger* is

   _____.

3. The words "do not like cubs" in paragraph 2 tell about the

   _____ _____.

4. The story does not say so, but it makes you think that
   a. most young animals are well taken care of.
   b. only wolves know how to care for their young properly.
   c. young animals must care for themselves.

5. The female stickleback fish
   a. builds a nest.   c. guards the nest.
   b. lays the eggs.   d. watches over the young.

6. Young stickleback fish never try to leave their nests.
       Yes   No   Does not say

7. On the whole, this story is about
   a. wild animals.
   b. animal parents.
   c. bears and fish.

8. How do wolves care for their young? (Check the story again.)
   a. They leave them alone.
   b. Both parents feed and watch over them.
   c. Only the female wolf protects the young.

9. Which of these sentences do you think is right?
   a. All animals of one kind live together as families.
   b. All young animals are cared for by their mothers.
   c. Young animals are cared for in different ways.

Animal Games

1   Children around the world like to play games. But did you know that many animals play games, too? Some of these games are almost like those you play.

2   In the winter, otters coast on ice. When they find a snowbank, they stop and slide down it again and again. In the summer, otters have just as much fun. They make their slides on the banks of rivers and ponds.

3   Some animals like to sing and dance in groups. Wolves gather on a hill when the moon is out and make a chorus as they howl together. Chimpanzees like to march in single file. They keep in step as they march around. Each chimpanzee comes down hard on one foot. Then, in a kind of rhythm, they shake their heads.

4   Other animals have favorite games like tag. Some kinds of fish and birds play follow-the-leader. English badgers play king-of-the castle. At sundown, the badgers go to the stump of a fallen tree. When one badger climbs to the top, the others try to climb up, too, and pull down the king.

1. In the winter, otters coast on
   a. river banks.   c. logs.
   b. ice.   d. sleds.

2. The word in paragraph 3 that means *to cry long and loudly* is

   _____.

3. The words "march in single file" in paragraph 3 refer to

   _____.

4. The story does not say so, but it makes you think that
   a. animals play games with children.
   b. animals learn to play games by watching children.
   c. some kinds of animals seem to have favorite games.

5. English badgers play
   a. tag.   c. marching games.
   b. follow-the-leader. d. king-of-the-castle.

6. Cats and dogs also have favorite games.
   Yes   No   Does not say

7. On the whole, this story is about
   a. games animals play.
   b. how animals hunt.
   c. singing and dancing.

8. Animals seem to play games in order to
   a. stay awake during the day.
   b. have fun like children.
   c. practice being children.

9. Which of these sentences do you think is right?
   a. Animals play games by themselves.
   b. Animals play games in groups.
   c. All animals play the same games.

"Fly Home with Me"

1   If your mother wants to tell you something, she uses words. Birds cannot talk as we do. But some birds can make sounds to warn their young of danger. They have their own ways to make the young birds do certain things.

2   The jackdaw is a kind of blackbird that lives in Europe. Jackdaws live together in flocks. Young jackdaws do not know their enemies. When an older jackdaw sees a dog, it makes a loud, rattling sound. The younger birds know this sound means an enemy is nearby. The sound warns them and teaches them to know their enemies.

3   If a young jackdaw is in a dangerous place, a jackdaw parent flies over him from behind. The parent bird flies low over the young bird's back. The parent's tail feathers move quickly from side to side. It is trying to say, "Follow me."

4   At the same time, the parent calls out, "Key-aw, key-aw." The parent means, "Fly home with me." The younger bird then follows the older one home.

5   Young jackdaws do not have to learn what certain sounds mean. They know the meaning of these sounds from the time they hatch.

1. The jackdaw lives in
   - a. America.
   - b. Europe.
   - c. Africa.
   - d. Australia.

2. The word in paragraph 2 that means *groups of birds* is

   _____.

3. The words "a kind of blackbird" in paragraph 2 refer to the

   _____.

4. The story does not say so, but it makes you think that
   - a. jackdaws have to be taught to know their enemies.
   - b. birds do not have their own language.
   - c. jackdaws have to learn what certain sounds mean.

5. When an older jackdaw sees a dog, it
   - a. flies away.
   - b. fights the dog.
   - c. calls out, "Follow me."
   - d. makes a loud sound.

6. Parent jackdaws can use their tail feathers to warn of danger.
   Yes   No   Does not say

7. On the whole, this story is about
   - a. ways in which people can talk to birds.
   - b. the nests of jackdaws.
   - c. the way jackdaws warn their young of danger.

8. Why did the parent jackdaw signal, "Fly home with me"? (Check the story again.)
   - a. Danger was near.
   - b. It was time to eat.
   - c. The parent was playing a game.

9. Which of these sentences do you think is right?
   - a. All animal parents can talk to their young.
   - b. The dog is not an enemy of the jackdaw.
   - c. Birds can give certain information to one another.

The World's Farmers

1   Farmland is very important to every country in the world. Farmland supplies the food needed by people everywhere. Who owns this land?

2   Farmland may be owned by the farmers who work the land. It may be owned by people who have others farm it. In some places, a government owns the farmland.

3   In England, many farmers rent their land. Some families have farmed a piece of land for generations without owning it.

4   In Chile, most farmland was once owned by a few wealthy landowners. Workers farmed the land for them. But, during the 1940s, many landowners divided their land into small farms and sold it. Today, there are fewer large farms but many smaller ones.

5   In Russia, all land belongs to the government. Almost all farmland is divided into group farms. Groups of workers live and work on the farms. Each worker receives some share of the crops.

6   In the United States, two-thirds of our land is made up of farms. Most farmland is owned by the families who farm the land. Only a few farmers rent their land from others. In the 1960s, 80 out of every 100 farmers owned the land they farmed.

FIND THE ANSWERS

1. Farmland supplies
   a. farms.
   b. food.
   c. farmers.
   d. landowners.

2. The word in paragraph 2 that means *to get land ready to plant crops*
   is _____.

3. The words "two-thirds of our land is made up of farms" in paragraph 6
   refer to the _____ _____.

4. The story does not say so, but it makes you think that
   a. everyone owns his own farmland.
   b. farmers cannot own land in some countries.
   c. farming is not important in our country.

5. In Chile during the 1940s many landowners
   a. divided their farms.
   b. gave their farms away.
   c. ran out of money.
   d. built factories on their land.

6. Most farmers rent their land.
   Yes   No   Does not say

7. On the whole, this story is about
   a. 100 farmers.
   b. different countries in Asia.
   c. owning farmland.

8. Why is farmland important all over the world? (Check the story again.)
   a. Farmers work the land to supply people with food.
   b. Most people visit farms during their summer vacations.
   c. It is where new cities will be built.

9. Which of these sentences do you think is right?
   a. English farm families move often.
   b. Farmlands are owned in different ways in different countries.
   c. Small farms are best.

The Outback

1   In the United States, there are different kinds of farmland. The land is planted with crops in many places. Only in the western part of our country do we have dry rangeland where cattle are raised.

2   But most of Australia's farmland has a dry climate similar to our rangeland. Less than 20 inches of rain fall each year. The land does not get enough rain for farmers to grow crops. So most farmland in Australia is used to raise sheep and cattle. Australia raises more sheep than any other country in the world.

3   In Australia, all large cities are on the coast. The people of Australia call the empty inland regions of their country the "outback." In the outback are huge sheep and cattle ranches called "stations." One station may cover thousands of miles.

4   The men and women of the outback are like the pioneers who first settled the American West. Some families live 400 miles from the nearest town. Herds going to market are driven hundreds of miles to the nearest railroad.

5   Sometimes it does not rain for years. The temperatures can go as high as 130°. These outback families often lead hard and lonely lives.

1. The outback has
   - a. jungles.
   - b. many large rivers.
   - c. high temperatures.
   - d. freezing winds.

2. The word in paragraph 3 that means *very big* or *very large* is

   _____.

3. The words "empty inland regions" in paragraph 3 refer to the word

   _____.

4. The story does not say so, but it makes you think that
   - a. few people live in the outback.
   - b. outback stations are always near railroads.
   - c. American pioneers moved to Australia.

5. Most farmland in Australia is used to raise
   - a. crops.
   - b. sheep and cattle.
   - c. kangaroos.
   - d. corn and potatoes.

6. The United States raises more sheep than any other country.
   Yes   No   Does not say

7. On the whole, this story is about
   - a. growing crops in Australia.
   - b. railroads in Australia.
   - c. farmland in Australia.

8. Why are sheep and cattle raised in the outback? (Check the story again.)
   - a. The people who live there don't know how to raise crops.
   - b. Sheep and cattle are easy to raise.
   - c. The land is too dry to grow crops.

9. Which of these sentences do you think is right?
   - a. Life in the outback is easy.
   - b. Families in the outback have to get along on their own.
   - c. It rains often in the outback and causes flooding.

Fewer Farmers But More Food

1   Today, most Americans live in cities and towns. People who live in cities do not raise their own food. Instead, they depend on our farmers for it.

2   In the 1800s, there were fewer people in the United States. However, more people were farmers then. In the 1900s, many people left their farms to work in big cities. Now fewer than 8 out of every 100 Americans live on farms.

3   Although there are fewer farmers, there are larger farms. In 1900, the average farm covered 150 acres. The average farmer in the 1960s owned 320 acres of land. Farmers can raise more crops now with the help of science and modern machines.

4   In the dry parts of the country, farmers can water their crops through irrigation. They can buy machines that will help them do their work. They can even go to school to learn how to be better farmers.

5   New machines and new ideas have helped the farmer in another way. Now farmers in the United States produce more food than ever before. In 1820, one farm worker could feed himself or herself and three other people. In the 1960s, a farm worker could grow enough food for thirty people.

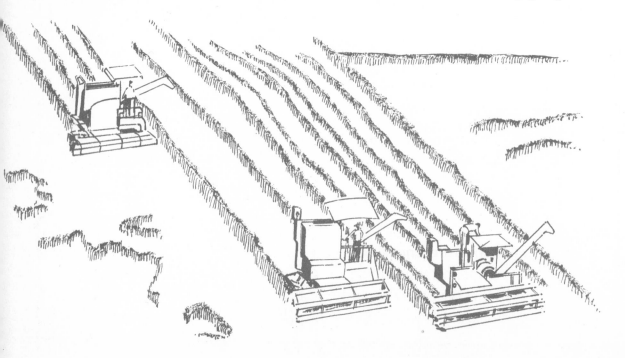

1. Farmers today
   a. live in towns and cities.
   c. grow more food.
   b. have less land.
   d. feed only themselves.

2. The word in paragraph 4 that means *the watering of crops* is

   _____.

3. The words "produce more food" in paragraph 5 refer to the

   _____.

4. The story does not say so, but it makes you think that
   a. ways of farming have changed.
   b. the people of today eat more.
   c. farmers cannot grow enough food to feed everyone.

5. In the 1960s, a farm worker could grow enough food for
   a. thirty people.
   c. twenty people.
   b. three people.
   d. thirteen people.

6. Farmers can grow more crops with the help of modern machines.
   Yes   No   Does not say

7. On the whole, this story is about
   a. farmers in the 1800s.
   b. going to school.
   c. modern farmers.

8. Why do people who live in cities depend on farmers for food? (Check the story again.)
   a. They do not raise their own food.
   b. They do not like the food that is grown in cities.
   c. Food produced by farmers is cheaper.

9. Which of these sentences do you think is right?
   a. We need more farmers in the United States.
   b. Farmers produce more food with the help of modern machines.
   c. Farms today are smaller than they used to be.

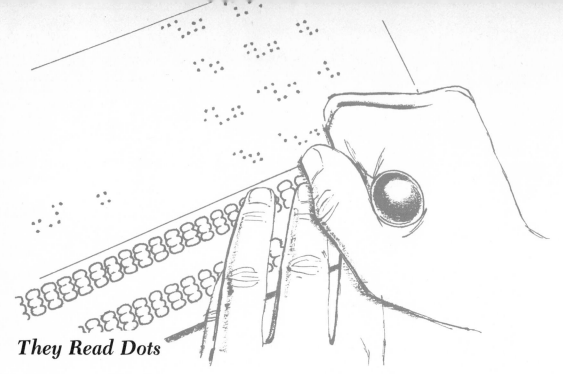

They Read Dots

1   To read this page, you must use your eyes. The blind can read, too, but they must use their fingers.

2   Over 100 years ago in France, a young boy was playing in his father's workshop. He was making holes in a piece of leather with a pointed tool. All at once, the tool flew from his hands and struck his face. This child, Louis Braille, had injured his eyes. Soon he was blind.

3   In those days, few blind people could read. Then, years later, Louis Braille had an idea. He remembered the holes he had once made in leather. If he pushed the tool only part way through the leather, he could feel raised dots on the other side. Using from one to five raised dots, he made up an alphabet.

4   Although only fifteen, Louis Braille had found a way for the blind to read. He had invented a kind of code that the fingers and the mind could learn. Named after its inventor, this new way to read was called Braille.

5   Today, many books are printed in Braille. Look below. Imagine that the dots are raised. Do you think your fingers could learn Braille?

a b c d e f g h i j k l m

n o p q r s t u v w x y z

FIND THE ANSWERS

1. People who read Braille
   a. have poor hearing.   c. are blind.
   b. can't read English.   d. have good eyesight.

2. The word in paragraph 2 that means *hurt* or *harmed* is

   is _____.

3. The words "new way to read" in paragraph 4 tell about the word

   _____.

4. The story does not say so, but it makes you think that
   a. few blind people can learn Braille.
   b. many blind people can learn Braille.
   c. anyone can read Braille.

5. The Braille alphabet is made up of
   a. round letters.   c. thin lines.
   b. raised dots.   d. square holes.

6. Louis Braille found a way for blind to read.
   Yes   No   Does not say

7. On the whole, this story is about
   a. making holes in leather.
   b. Louis Braille and an alphabet.
   c. using your eyes to read faster.

8. How does Braille help the blind? (Check the story again.)
   a. It gives them a way to read.
   b. It gives their fingers something to do.
   c. It helps them work with leather.

9. Which of these sentences do you think is right?
   a. Young children should not play with leather.
   b. Braille is read with the toes.
   c. Before Braille, few blind people could read.

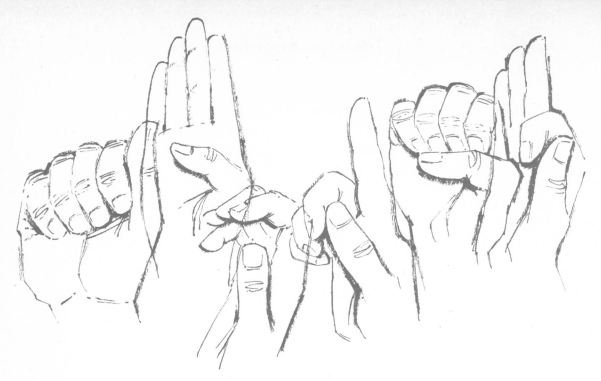

They Speak with Their Hands

1   For many years, no one could communicate with people who had been born without hearing. These deaf people were not able to use a spoken language.

2   But, beginning in the 1700s, the deaf were taught a special language. Using this language, they could share thoughts and ideas with others. The language they used was a language without sound. It was a sign language.

3   How did this sign language work? The deaf were taught to make certain movements using their hands, faces, and bodies. These movements stood for things and ideas. People might move their forefingers across their lips. This meant, "You are not telling the truth." They might tap their chins with three fingers. This meant "my uncle."

4   The deaf were also taught to use a finger alphabet. They used their fingers to make the letters of the alphabet. In this way, they spelled out words. Some deaf people could spell out words at a speed of 130 words per minute.

5   Sign language and finger spelling are not used as much as they once were. Today, the deaf are taught to understand others by watching their lips. They are also taught how to speak.

1. In the 1700s, the deaf were taught
    - a. to speak.
    - b. to watch others.
    - c. sign language.
    - d. Braille.

2. The word in paragraph 3 that means *the finger next to the thumb* is

    _____ .

3. The words "a language without sound" in paragraph 2 tell about a

    _____ _____ .

4. The story does not say so, but it makes you think that
    - a. the deaf must have special teachers.
    - b. there is still no way to communicate with the deaf.
    - c. deaf people make signs to earn a living.

5. A tap on the chin with three fingers means
    - a. "hello."
    - b. "come here."
    - c. "I have a toothache."
    - d. "my uncle."

6. Sign language is used as much today as it once was.

    Yes   No   Does not say

7. On the whole, this story is about
    - a. how the deaf communicate.
    - b. learning to spell.
    - c. teaching the deaf to speak.

8. How did sign language help the deaf? (Check the story again.)
    - a. It helped them learn to read.
    - b. The deaf could understand Indian sign language.
    - c. It helped them communicate with other people.

9. Which of these sentences do you think is right?
    - a. Deaf people draw signs.
    - b. Deaf people read with their fingers.
    - c. Many deaf people now can speak.

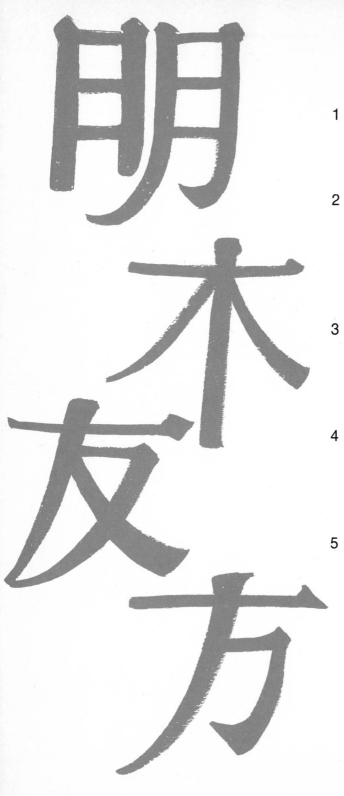

They Read Pictures

1 The Chinese began writing their language over 3,000 years ago. Their way of writing is very different from ours.

2 Until a few years ago, the Chinese did not have an alphabet. Their language was written in characters. These characters were a little like pictures. Each one stood for a different word.

3 Probably the first characters had been pictures. The character for "sun" was a circle with a dot in the center. The character for "man" looked like a body with two legs.

4 As time went on, the characters changed. New ones were added. A person could no longer tell what a character meant just by looking at it.

5 In order to read or write, people had to learn thousands of characters. Even to read a newspaper, they had to know 2,000 different characters. Learning so many characters was difficult. Many people in China could not read or write. In fact, there were letter writers in front of Chinese post offices. These people sat at tables and were paid to write letters for others.

1. The first Chinese characters were probably
   a. letters.   c. people.
   b. circles.   d. pictures.

2. The word in paragraph 3 that means *no doubt* or *it was likely* is

   _____.

3. The words "a little like pictures" in paragraph 2 refers to the word

   _____.

4. The story does not say so, but it makes you think that
   a. few Chinese wrote their own letters.
   b. the Chinese alphabet is very old.
   c. it is easy to read a Chinese newspaper.

5. Learning many Chinese characters was
   a. difficult.   c. fun.
   b. silly.   d. easy.

6. The character for "sun" was a square.
   Yes   No   Does not say

7. On the whole, this story is about
   a. Chinese post offices.
   b. Chinese characters.
   c. characters in a play.

8. Why did the Chinese need to know so many characters to write? (Check the story again.)
   a. Chinese has more words than other languages.
   b. Each character stood for a different word.
   c. They liked to write long letters.

9. Which of these sentences do you think is right?
   a. Chinese characters looked more like drawings than letters.
   b. The Chinese invented an alphabet hundreds of years ago.
   c. Chinese characters did not change through the years.

A Noisy Dance

1   Young people in most countries like to dance. Different peoples have different kinds of dances.

2   Pretend that you are in Africa. You are visiting the Kikuyu (kə kü′ yü) tribe.

3   Hear the drums beat! Listen to the flutes! Almost 2,000 Kikuyus are meeting for the most important dance of the year.

4   First, the Kikuyus choose a large, flat place for their dance. For hundreds of years, they have danced on a fall night when the moon is full. The moon and the glow from small fires light the dancers.

5   Older people watch from the side while young men and women gather at the dancing place. The girls wear beaded leather skirts and tops. The men wear fancy headdresses and carry spears. The dancers' skin and clothes are colored by light red chalk. The chalk and the firelight make the dancers look like statues.

6   The dancers act out stories of good and bad deeds. The dances tell stories of lion hunts and other adventures. In one dance, the girls stand on the boys' feet. The girls are pretending to be afraid of snakes.

7   All night the drums beat and the fires burn. But the dancers never seem to get tired.

1. The place where the Kikuyu tribe dances is
   a. flat.   c. hilly.
   b. small.   d. square.

2. The word in paragraph 2 that means *make believe* is

   _____.

3. The words "look like statues" in paragraph 5 describe the

   _____.

4. The story does not say so, but it makes you think that
   a. few people go to Kikuyu dances.
   b. the Kikuyu dance is an old custom.
   c. the Kikuyu girls and boys dance to band music.

5. The dancers' skin and clothes are covered with
   a. paint.   c. feathers.
   b. dust.   d. chalk.

6. The dancing area is lit by electric lights.
   Yes   No   Does not say

7. On the whole, this story is about
   a. the beat of drums.
   b. an African dance.
   c. African storytelling.

8. What do the Kikuyu dances tell? (Check the story again.)
   a. The dances tell the story of drum beats.
   b. The dances tell about adventures.
   c. The dances tell funny jokes.

9. Which of these sentences do you think is right?
   a. The Kikuyus do not often get together.
   b. Dancing is important to the Kikuyus.
   c. The most important event is a singing group.

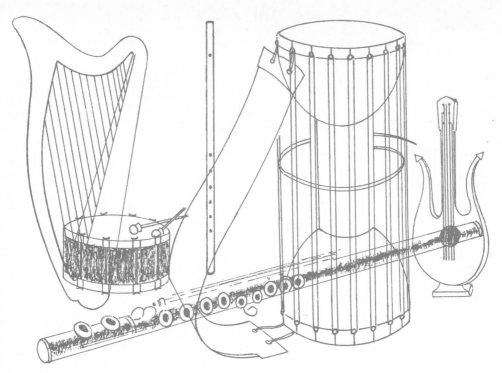

Harps, Flutes, and Drums

1   People from all countries have played musical instruments at some time in their history. But not all people have made music in the same way. Old musical instruments were many and different. There were rattles to shake and flutes to blow. There were drums to beat and harps to strum.

2   In the Middle East, people played instruments with strings. Their first stringed instrument was a hunting bow. People played tunes on it by using the bow string. From the musical bow was to come the idea for the harp.

3   Long ago in Greece, people made music by blowing into a hollow reed or pipe called a flute. The flute was a very popular instrument. It was played during boxing matches and foot races. And on Greek ships, flute players kept time for the men rowing.

4   In Africa, the most important musical instrument was the drum. Hundreds of years ago, the Africans learned to make drums by stretching animal skins over hollow logs. They used drums to keep time as they danced. They also beat out codes on their drums. In this way, they sent messages through the jungle.

1. Instruments with strings were played in
   - a. Africa.
   - b. Greece.
   - c. the Middle East.
   - d. South America.

2. The word in paragraph 1 that means *something that music is played on*

   is _____.

3. The words "first stringed instrument" in paragraph 2 refer to the

   _____ _____.

4. The story does not say so, but it makes you think that
   - a. people all over the world like music.
   - b. everyone plays the same kind of instrument.
   - c. drummers kept time for the men rowing.

5. Drums were made from
   - a. hunting bows.
   - b. empty gourds.
   - c. hollow reeds.
   - d. hollow logs.

6. The idea for the harp came from the musical bow.
   Yes   No   Does not say

7. On the whole, this story is about
   - a. stretching animal skins.
   - b. sending messages.
   - c. musical instruments.

8. How was the flute played? (Check the story again.)
   - a. It was played by hitting the strings.
   - b. It was played by blowing on a hollow reed.
   - c. It was played by shaking and beating the instrument.

9. Which of these sentences do you think is right?
   - a. Different peoples often play different instruments.
   - b. Musical instruments have not changed over the years.
   - c. The Middle East has the best musical instruments.

A Different Kind of Play

1   Maybe your class in school has given a play. People throughout the world like to act in plays. In Japan, actors perform in Kabuki (kə bü′ kē) plays. The word is made up of three Japanese words meaning song, dance, and ability.

2   Kabuki actors do not look like the actors in American plays. American actors dress and look like real people. In Kabuki plays, the actors wear bright-colored robes and wigs. Their robes are very large, and their wigs do not look like real hair.

3   American actors wear make-up, but their make-up does not often hide their faces. Kabuki actors paint their faces chalk white. They draw black eyebrows above their real eyebrows. They outline their eyes in black or red. Their mouths are bright red. They look as if they are wearing masks.

4   An actor performing in an American play must make his face look happy, sad, or angry. Make-up helps the Kabuki actor show his feelings. If an actor is going to show anger, he paints dark blue or red lines on his face. His make-up makes him look angry.

5   American and Kabuki actors perform in different ways. But they both try to please the people who watch them.

1. Most Kabuki plays are given in
   a. China.   c. Korea.
   b. Japan.   d. India.

2. The word in paragraph 1 that means *to act* is _____.

3. The words "look as if they are wearing masks" in paragraph 3 refer to

   _____ _____.

4. The story does not say so, but it makes you think that
   a. Kabuki actors are afraid to show their real faces.
   b. American actors don't wear make-up.
   c. make-up helps a Kabuki actor look sad.

5. To show anger, a Kabuki actor paints
   a. dark lines on his face.   c. his costume blue.
   b. hair on his head.   d. his eyebrows black.

6. Kabuki actors wear bright-colored robes and wigs.
   Yes   No   Does not say

7. On the whole, this story is about
   a. how the Japanese sing and dance.
   b. why actors look sad or happy.
   c. a kind of Japanese play.

8. Why do Kabuki actors wear so much make-up? (Check the story again.)
   a. They do not want anyone to know who they are.
   b. It helps them show their feelings during a play.
   c. They think it makes them look better.

9. Which of these sentences do you think is right?
   a. Americans are not used to seeing Kabuki plays.
   b. Kabuki actors and American actors are much the same.
   c. American actors wear more make-up than Kabuki actors.

A Warm Air Bath

1   In Finland, most houses have a sauna (sô′ nə). The sauna is a small wood hut or a room with a furnace inside. Stones piled over the furnace are heated red-hot. After the stones are heated, the sauna is used for taking a sauna bath.

2   The temperature in the sauna is sometimes over 190 degrees. People taking a sauna bath sit or lie on a wood platform in the hot, dry air. The hot air makes them perspire. From time to time, they pour water on the hot stones to make clouds of steam.

3   People in the sauna beat themselves with branches from a birch tree. They do this to make themselves perspire more. Then they wash with soap and water. After washing, they cool off in cold water.

4   The sauna is often built near a lake, and people go from the hot sauna into the cool water. If it is winter, they may roll in the snow. After cooling off, they rest.

5   In Finland, most families take a sauna bath at least once a week. For Finns, the sauna bath is more than a way to get clean. It is a way to relax and enjoy themselves.

FIND THE ANSWERS

1. The Finns often build saunas near a lake because they
   a. do not like to walk far.   c. can get a drink there.
   b. cool off in the water.   d. think lakes are beautiful.

2. The word in paragraph 3 that means *to give off liquid through the skin*

   is _____.

3. The words "heated red-hot" in paragraph 1 refer to the

   _____.

4. The story does not say so, but it makes you think that the sauna
   a. is important to the Finns.
   b. is a waste of time.
   c. is used only in the winter.

5. The temperature in the sauna is
   a. as cold as snow.   c. below zero.
   b. the same as the temperature   d. warmer than a hot day.
   outside.

6. The Finns also have bathtubs.
   Yes   No   Does not say

7. On the whole, this story is about
   a. rolling in the snow.
   b. the sauna bath.
   c. birch branches.

8. People in a sauna beat themselves with birch branches in order to
   a. make themselves perspire more.
   b. stop the itching caused by the heat.
   c. punish themselves.

9. Which of these sentences do you think is right?
   a. The sauna is in a special building or room.
   b. People take a sauna bath to get warm.
   c. People take a sauna bath because they have nothing else to do.

The Siesta

1   In Mexico, people stop working for two hours in the afternoon. Mexicans eat a big lunch and visit with friends. They may have time to lie in a hammock and enjoy a quiet rest.

2   The custom of resting in the afternoon is an old one. The weather in Mexico is very warm. Many years ago, people could not work outside in the middle of the day. It was too hot. They had a time of rest at midday called the siesta (sē es′ tə). Now, many people work in air-conditioned buildings, but everyone still takes time off from work at midday.

3   In Mexico lunch is the biggest meal of the day. Most people who work in offices have two hours for lunch. There are few quick-lunch counters to visit for a fast snack. If people do not want to go home, they eat in a hotel or restaurant. Most people go home for lunch so the whole family can eat together. Sometimes there are guests, too.

4   Mexicans want a long lunchtime. They do not like to hurry. They want to enjoy the meal and to visit with family and friends. They want time for a siesta.

FIND THE ANSWERS

1. A Mexican eats a lunch that is
   - a. small.
   - b. big.
   - c. fast.
   - d. just a snack.

2. The word in paragraph 1 that means *a hanging canvas bed* is

   _____.

3. The words "a time of rest at midday" in paragraph 2 refer to the

   _____.

4. The story does not say so, but it makes you think that
   - a. there are many people in Mexico who do not go home for lunch.
   - b. going home for lunch is important to a Mexican.
   - c. Mexicans are in a hurry at lunchtime.

5. In Mexico the biggest meal of the day is
   - a. breakfast.
   - b. an evening snack.
   - c. dinner.
   - d. lunch.

6. There are many quick-service lunch counters in Mexico.
   - Yes   No   Does not say

7. On the whole, this story is about
   - a. Mexican food.
   - b. the weather in Mexico.
   - c. lunchtime in Mexico.

8. Why do the Mexicans like to have a long lunchtime? (Check the story again.)
   - a. They don't like to work in air-conditioned buildings.
   - b. They like time to visit with their family and friends.
   - c. It takes a long time to eat the many foods that are served.

9. Which of these sentences do you think is right?
   - a. Mexicans do not like to eat quick lunches.
   - b. Even with air-conditioning, it is too hot to work in Mexico.
   - c. Mexican families do not often eat together.

Beautiful Parks

1   As our cities grow bigger, more land is taken up by buildings. For miles on each side of many big cities, buildings take the place of trees.

2   But even people who live in cities can enjoy America's parks and forests. Found in different parts of America, these parks are owned by our government. No one can build houses or stores there. The parks are kept so that people can hike, camp, and picnic. They can relax there.

3   One of the most popular American parks is Yellowstone National Park in the Northwest. It is the oldest of all the parks owned by the government. In 1872, it was set aside for the people to enjoy. Each year, thousands of people come to Yellowstone. They see high mountains, beautiful waterfalls, and thousands of hot water springs called geysers. Yellowstone has more geysers than all the rest of the world together.

4   Forests were not always open to all the people. In England long ago, the forests belonged to the king. It was against the law for the people to go there.

5   Most people in America like to go to parks. They are glad that their parks are kept open for everyone to use and enjoy.

1. Near many cities, buildings take the place of
      a. streets.   c. trees.
      b. geysers.   d. parks.

2. The word in paragraph 2 that means *to be happy with* or *to like to use* is _____.

3. The words "one of the most popular American parks" in paragraph 3 refer to _____ _____ _____.

4. The story does not say so, but it makes you think that
      a. England does not have parks.
      b. there are few parks in America.
      c. parks often have trees.

5. Yellowstone has many
      a. cities.   c. buildings.
      b. stores.   d. geysers.

6. Forests in England once belonged to the king.
      Yes   No   Does not say

7. On the whole, this story is about
      a. big cities.
      b. parks and forests.
      c. American cities.

8. The government has set aside land to be kept as parks in order to
      a. stop building.
      b. let people relax somewhere.
      c. help keep cities small.

9. Which of these sentences do you think is right?
      a. The United States is the only country that has parks.
      b. People do not often visit Yellowstone.
      c. It is important to have parks that everyone can use.

Magic Machines

1   Fifty years ago, one farm worker could grow enough food to feed seven people. Today, one worker can feed thirty people. What made the difference?

2   Modern machines have changed farming. It once took many workers many hours to pick a cherry orchard in Michigan. Now some farmers are using new cherry-picking machines. These machines shake the trees, catch the fruit in heavy cloth sheets, and push the cherries along belts. They are then dumped into huge tubs of water. Only two people and one machine are needed for a whole orchard. It takes just three minutes to pick each tree.

3   Other machines shake trees and catch nut and plum crops. Machines are also used to harvest cotton, corn, oats, and barley.

4   Another new machine picks tomatoes. First, it cuts the vine below the ground. Then the vines and tomatoes are pulled inside the machine. Finally, it separates the fruit from the vines and returns the vines to the field.

5   It will soon be possible for powerful wind machines to blow oranges off trees. New machines now being tested will pick peaches, blueberries, plums, cooking apples, and strawberries.

1. Fifty years ago, one farm worker could grow enough food to feed
   a. many people.   c. seven people.
   b. an army.   d. thirty people.

2. The word in paragraph 2 that means *a place where many fruit trees are grown* is _____.

3. The words "blow oranges off trees" in paragraph 5 refer to

   _____.

4. The story does not say so, but it makes you think that
   a. modern machines help people to work faster.
   b. modern machines need many people to work them.
   c. one machine can be used to harvest many kinds of crops.

5. New machines are being tested to pick
   a. cherries.   c. oats.
   b. plums.   d. potatoes.

6. There is a machine now used to pick pears.
   Yes   No   Does not say

7. On the whole, this story is about
   a. cherry orchards.
   b. tomato-picking machines.
   c. modern farm machinery.

8. How have modern machines changed farming? (Check the story again.)
   a. They make farming harder.
   b. It is now possible for one machine to run a farm.
   c. They make harvesting crops easier and faster.

9. Which of these sentences do you think is right?
   a. Modern farm machines are a great help to the farmer.
   b. The new machines pull up fruit trees.
   c. Modern machines help the wind blow.

From Farm to Family

1   Everyone knows cows give milk. But did you know that machines get the milk from farm to family?

2   At one time, a farmer had to milk his cows by hand. Today, many farmers have electric milking machines to do the work for them. A milking machine can milk two or more cows at one time. And it does the job in a matter of minutes.

3   From the milking machine, the milk flows through pipes into a big metal tank. There, the milk is kept cool until a large tank truck stops at the farm. The tank truck can hold 2,000 gallons of milk and keep it cold. The tank truck may go to a dairy more than 100 miles away.

4   At the dairy, the milk is heated to kill germs. It is also put into bottles. Bottling machines do the work of many hands. They wash and scrub thousands of bottles inside and out. When the bottles are clean, they are carried on a moving belt to a bottle-filling machine. This machine fills each bottle with the right amount of milk. Then it puts on the cap.

5   Other machines put milk into paper cartons. After the milk has been put into bottles or cartons, it is ready for your family.

1. Milking machines are run by
    a. hand.   c. electricity.
    b. germs.   d. cows.

2. The word in paragraph 3 that means *measures of a liquid* is

    _____.

3. The words "They wash and scrub thousands of bottles" in paragraph 4

    refer to the _____ _____.

4. The story does not say so, but it makes you think that
    a. machines help keep milk free of germs.
    b. cows are afraid of milking machines.
    c. milk can be made by machines.

5. Tank trucks pick up milk at the
    a. factory.   c. store.
    b. farm.   d. machine.

6. Machines get the milk ready for the family.
    Yes   No   Does not say

7. On the whole, this story is about
    a. how much milk cows give.
    b. tank trucks.
    c. milk and machines.

8. What happens to the milk when it is in a big metal tank? (Check the
    story again.)
    a. It is kept warm.
    b. It is kept cool.
    c. It is made into ice cream.

9. Which of these sentences do you think is right?
    a. Machines are important in getting milk to your kitchen.
    b. Milk is made at the dairy by many machines.
    c. Milk is ready for your family when it comes from the cow.

Please Pass the Potato Chips!

1   Americans buy more than 600 million bags of potato chips each year. If people had to make potato chips in their own kitchens, they might not eat so many.

2   From field to factory, potato chips are made by machines. A machine digs the potatoes in the field. A second machine puts them in sacks. A truck takes them to the factory. There, they are fed into a peeling machine. They are tumbled over rough machinery that scrapes away the skins.

3   The next machine cuts the potatoes into slices, which are washed in cold water. The slices are cooked in hot oil in a frying machine.

4   The potatoes turn a golden color. They are now thin chips that ride along on a moving steel belt. Salt is sprinkled on them from above. Any chips that are broken or too brown are removed. The finished chips go into a machine that makes bags and puts in the chips. This machine also weighs and seals the bags.

5   When you put your hand into the bag, you are the first to touch the chips. Machines have done all the work.

1. The machine that is used in potato fields
   a. takes the potatoes to the factory.
   b. cuts the potatoes into pieces.
   c. digs the potatoes.
   d. peels the potatoes.

2. The word in paragraph 2 that means *not smooth* is _____.

3. The words "weighs and seals the bags" in paragraph 4 tell about the word _____.

4. The story does not say so, but it makes you think that
   a. potato chips are washed just before they go into bags.
   b. potato chips are made by hand.
   c. potato chips are a favorite American snack.

5. The golden potato chips ride along on a belt made of
   a. rubber.
   b. paper.
   c. wood.
   d. steel.

6. Potatoes are sliced in the field.
   Yes   No   Does not say

7. On the whole, this story is about
   a. making potato chips.
   b. digging potatoes.
   c. how potato chips are sorted.

8. Why are potato chips made by machines? (Check the story again.)
   a. It is a faster way to make millions of chips.
   b. Workers would break too many of the potato chips.
   c. Workers would eat too many of the chips.

9. Which of these sentences do you think is right?
   a. Potato chips are made from the skins of potatoes.
   b. Potato chips are cooked in hot water.
   c. Several machines are used in making potato chips.

Money That Works

1   You may put your money in a box or a jar at your home to keep it safe. Or you may want to put your money in a large bank. The bank not only keeps your money safe but also sends it out to work.

2   The bank will give people money for a special reason. This is called a *loan*. A family may wish to buy a new car, but they do not have enough money. So they will ask the bank for a loan. The bank will give the family enough money to buy a car. Later they will pay it back to the bank.

3   Doris Vierheller is president of the only bank in Lebanon, Illinois. Most of the loans that she makes in Lebanon will be for a new house, a car, or even a vacation.

4   Janice Notaro, vice president of a bank in Los Angeles, California, might loan money to build a new hospital.

5   Dorothy Ryan is a member of the board of directors of a large bank in New York City. Her bank might loan money to a company in Argentina to build a big new ship.

6   Your money might be sent to work all over the world. But it will always be there when you want it back.

1. When banks give money for special reasons, it is called a
   a. check.   c. credit.
   b. loan.   d. budget.

2. The word in paragraph 2 that means *not usual* is _____.

3. The word "she" in paragraph 3 refers to _____.

4. The story does not say so, but it makes you think that
   a. banks never give people money.
   b. banks like hospitals.
   c. banks loan a lot of money.

5. Banks keep your money
   a. safe.   c. in a jar.
   b. in a box.   d. in a house.

6. Banks might loan money to build a hospital.
   Yes   No   Does not say

7. On the whole, the story is about
   a. shipbuilding.
   b. banking.
   c. vacations.

8. Why does a family ask for money for a car? (Check the story.)
   a. They want to take a trip.
   b. They do not have enough money to buy one.
   c. Their neighbors have a new car.

9. Which of these sentences do you think is right?
   a. Small cities do not have banks.
   b. Banks have large windows.
   c. Banks may loan money to another country.

Long-Headed Women

1   Each country has its own cus-toms. Some customs have to do with how people look. From early times, women have been inter-ested in how their hair looks.

2   The Mangbetu (mäng be′ tü′) are a tribe that lives in Africa. Long ago, the women in this tribe wanted to be long-headed. They thought long heads and fancy hair styles were beautiful. So they bound the heads of their baby girls.

3   Mangbetu mothers wrapped cord tightly around the back and top of their baby daughters' heads. The little girls looked as if they were wearing tight hats over their hair. As time went by, the girls' heads were shaped by the cord.

4   When the girls grew up, the tops of their heads stood high above their foreheads like hills. They were long-headed women.

5   Mangbetu women fixed their hair in fancy styles. It took many hours. Sometimes they pushed all their hair back and up to the tops of their heads. Their hair made a circle above their heads. Then their heads looked even longer.

110

1. The Mangbetu are a tribe living in
   - a. America.
   - b. a cold country.
   - c. the North.
   - d. Africa.

2. The word in paragraph 1 that means *habits* or *ways of doing things* is

   _____ .

3. The words "made a circle above their heads" in paragraph 5 tell about

   the Mangbetu women's _____ .

4. The story does not say so, but makes you think that binding heads
   - a. made girls sick.
   - b. made girls' heads smaller.
   - c. took a long time.

5. Mangbetu women were interested in their
   - a. hair.
   - b. skin.
   - c. feet.
   - d. clothes.

6. Mangbetu girls wore tight hats over their hair.
   Yes   No   Does not say

7. On the whole, this article is about
   - a. little girls' hats.
   - b. the custom of binding heads.
   - c. hills in Africa.

8. Why did the Mangbetu women bind their daughters' heads? (Check the story again.)
   - a. They thought the cord would keep off the hot sun.
   - b. They couldn't find anything else to do.
   - c. They thought it made the girls more beautiful.

9. Which of these sentences do you think is right?
   - a. Mangbetu babies were born with long heads.
   - b. The heads of all Mangbetu women looked something alike.
   - c. Mangbetu women did not fix their hair in fancy styles.

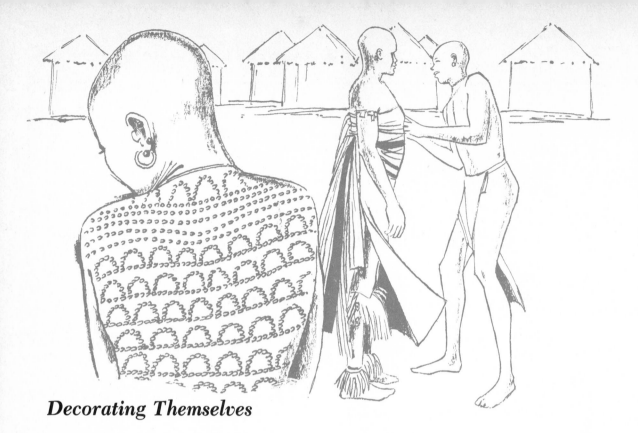

Decorating Themselves

1   When we want to look our best, we dress up in our nicest clothes. We are using the clothes to decorate ourselves.

2   The Nubas (nü′ bəz) in the African country of Sudan do not wear clothes. They use another kind of decoration. They have scars which form designs on their skin.

3   You may wonder how a Nuba gets these scars. First, a design is cut into the skin. Then a kind of oil is rubbed into the wounds. When the wounds heal, scars are left. The scars rise in bumps above the skin and form designs.

4   The scarring of a Nuba girl begins when she is seven or eight. Sometimes a woman's entire body is covered by designs.

5   The Nuba men also decorate themselves. In fact, they keep the most beautiful designs for themselves. Their cuts are deeper, so their scars stand out more.

6   The Nubas use many different designs, and some are favorites. A young woman likes to have three rows of scars across her left shoulder. A Nuba man sometimes has the figure of an animal carved on his chest.

7   The Nubas are proud of their decorations. They want to look their best.

1. The Nubas decorate themselves with
    a. scars.   c. beads.
    b. clothes.   d. fancy hats.

2. The word in paragraph 3 that means *stand up* is _____.

3. The words "form designs on their skin" in paragraph 2 refer to the
   Nubas' _____.

4. The story does not say so, but it makes you think that
    a. women have more designs than young girls.
    b. men do not scar themselves.
    c. all the scars are made at one time.

5. The Nubas make designs on their
    a. clothes.   c. shirts.
    b. skin.   d. houses.

6. The Sudan is in Africa.
    Yes   No   Does not say

7. On the whole, this story is about
    a. long-headed women.
    b. Nuba men.
    c. Nuba decorations.

8. Why do the Nubas scar themselves? (Check the story again.)
    a. They want to see who can make the best designs.
    b. It is the way to punish their children.
    c. They believe it makes them look their best.

9. Which of these sentences do you think is right?
    a. Nubas wear clothes that have fancy designs on them.
    b. People decorate themselves in different ways.
    c. Nuba men and women use the same designs.

The Hungry Cat
(An Indian Folktale)

A cat and a parrot were once good friends.

"You must come to my house for dinner," said the cat.

"Thank you," said the parrot. "Then you must be my guest for dinner."

When the parrot went to the cat's house, the cat prepared a very poor meal. There was nothing that the parrot liked, but he was too polite to say so.

Next, the cat went to the parrot's house for dinner. The parrot had worked all day. He roasted a big piece of meat. He had a pot of tea and a basket of fruit. He baked 500 little cakes with raisins in them.

The parrot put all the food before the cat except two little cakes with

114

raisins in them. He kept those for himself. "Two cakes are all I want," he said.

The cat gobbled up all her food. Then she said, "I'm hungry. Where is my dinner?"

The parrot tried to be polite. "You may have my two cakes with raisins in them."

The cat ate the cakes. "Is that all you have?" she asked.

"It is," said the angry parrot, "unless you wish to eat me!"

"All right," said the cat. And she ate the parrot.

An old woman had seen the whole thing. "Cat!" she called out. "You should not have eaten your friend!"

"Mind your own business," said the cat. "I think I will eat you, too." And she ate the old woman.

The cat walked down the road. She met a man and his donkey. "Out of my way, cat!" shouted the man. "My donkey may step on you!"

"What do I care?" said the cat. "I have just eaten 500 cakes, a parrot, and an old woman. I think I will eat you, too." And she ate both the man and the donkey and walked on.

The King and Queen were coming down the road. Behind them came all the soldiers and dozens of elephants marching two by two.

The happy King spoke kindly.

"Stand aside, pussy cat. My elephants might hurt you."

"Hurt *me*?" said the hungry cat. "I have just eaten 500 cakes, a parrot, an old woman, and a man and his donkey! I think I will eat you, too!" And the cat ate the King, the Queen, the soldiers, and all the elephants marching two by two.

The cat walked on, a little more slowly. She met two land crabs. They were walking sidewise in the dust, as crabs will do.

"Out of our way, Puss," said the land crabs.

"Out of *your* way?" said the cat. "I have just eaten 500 cakes, a parrot, an old woman, a man and his donkey, a King and Queen, all the soldiers, and his elephants marching two by two. I think I will eat you, too." And she ate the crabs.

When the land crabs were inside the cat, they looked around. It was very dark, but they could see the King holding the Queen's hand. The elephants were trying to line up two by two. The soldiers were stepping on each other's toes. The old woman was talking to the old man and the donkey. The parrot was sitting on a big pile of cakes with raisins in them.

The crabs cut a hole in the side of the cat with their sharp claws. They walked out sidewise, as crabs will

115

do. After them came the King, the Queen, the soldiers, the elephants marching two by two, the man and his donkey, the old woman and, last of all, the parrot. The parrot was carrying two cakes with raisins in them.

"Two cakes are all I want," he said.

The hungry cat went off to find a needle and thread to sew up the hole in her coat.

And that is why cats and parrots are no longer friends.

648 words

III

Communities Establish Patterns of Behavior

In this section you will read about how communities establish patterns of behavior. You will read about these things from the standpoint of history, biology, economics, sociology, art, geography, engineering, and anthropology.

Keep these questions in mind when you are reading.

1. What are some things that cause us to develop certain customs?

2. Are these things established quickly or slowly?

3. Are well-established customs always good?

4. How do customs affect us?

5. Is it good to study about other peoples? Why?

Separate Castes

1   Long ago, around 1500 B.C., warriors from the north came down into the country we now call India. They fought their way through mountain passes. Finally, these warriors, the Aryans (ãr′ ē ənz), became the rulers of the country.

2   The Aryans thought that they were more important than the people who had lost. So they kept their subjects separate from themselves.

3   They divided their subjects into four groups, or classes. The people in each class made their living in a different way. Some were religious leaders, and some were soldiers. Others were farmers. Most were workers. But each class was separate. It could have nothing to do with the other groups. The Aryans ruled over all the classes.

4   Separate classes became a part of Indian life. These classes were called castes (kasts). Indians of different castes could not eat or work together. They could not marry each other. The people believed that they were born into castes, and they could never leave them.

5   In some country villages in India, people still live this way. But there are modern Indians today who do not believe in castes. They are working to create a more open way of life for all people.

118

1. The Aryans came to India through
       a. heavy snows.   c. mountain passes.
       b. deep rivers.   d. separate classes.

2. The word in paragraph 5 that means *present day* or *not long ago* is

   _____.

3. The words "these warriors" in paragraph 1 refer to the _____.

4. The story does not say so, but it makes you think that
       a. the Aryans ruled over the American Indians.
       b. all modern Indians believe in separate castes.
       c. India is a very old country.

5. Aryan warriors came to India from the
       a. sea.   c. cities.
       b. north.   d. south.

6. The Aryans had a king.
       Yes   No   Does not say

7. On the whole, this story is about
       a. country villages.
       b. castes in India.
       c. Indians in the United States.

8. How were castes different from one another? (Check the story again.)
       a. One caste was made up of women and the others of men.
       b. All the tall people were in one caste and the short people in another.
       c. Each caste made their living in a different way.

9. Which of these sentences do you think is right?
       a. The caste system is very old, and it is hard to change.
       b. The Aryans were not important in the early history of India.
       c. All the people made their living in the same way.

Education for All

1   Today, all fifty states in America have many laws about education. One of these laws says all children must go to school. Each state collects tax money from people who own property. Taxes are used to build schools, buy books, and pay teachers. In that way, everyone can go to school.

2   In Colonial days, it was different. Usually, people had to pay to send children to school. Not everyone could afford to send their children, and many young people never went to school. In school, most children were taught only to read and write. Children from rich families had a better education.

3   During the early 1800s, people began to think it was important for all children to have an education. In 1852, Massachusetts passed a law which said that all children must go to school. Then other states passed education laws. At first, children only had to go to school four or five years. There were no high schools.

4   Now children must remain in school until they are sixteen. In some states, they must stay in school until they are eighteen. Schools are paid for by tax money. All children have a chance to learn.

1. In America, there are education laws
   a. nowhere.   c. in some states.
   b. in every state.   d. only in the East.

2. The word in paragraph 4 that means *stay* or *keep on* is _____.

3. The words "are paid for by tax money" in paragraph 4 tell about the word _____.

4. The story does not say so, but it makes you think that
   a. only a few children can go to school today.
   b. there are no education laws.
   c. Massachusetts was the first state to pass education laws.

5. In some states, children must stay in school until they are
   a. ten.   c. twenty-one.
   b. twelve.   d. eighteen.

6. Taxes pay teachers, buy books, and build schools.
   Yes   No   Does not say

7. On the whole, this story is about
   a. Massachusetts.
   b. education.
   c. property taxes.

8. Why did states pass laws saying that all children must go to school? (Check the story again.)
   a. They wanted children to stop bothering their mothers.
   b. They wanted to raise more taxes.
   c. They believed that all children should go to school.

9. Which of these sentences do you think is right?
   a. Children from poor families do not have a chance to learn.
   b. Education laws have not helped schools very much.
   c. Americans believe that education is important.

Trial by Jury

1   In the United States everyone has the right to a trial by jury. If a person is charged with a crime but says, "I am not guilty," there will be a trial. The person is brought before a jury made up of twelve people. The members of the jury listen to facts about the crime. They decide if the person is guilty or not guilty.

2   The earliest juries in England were used mostly to get facts about a crime. An English country-woman might see a thief stealing a sheep. She would tell the judge who the thief was. If the judge did not know the boundary line of the royal land, a member of the jury would go get the facts. These jury members were like witnesses or detectives.

3   In the 1100s, trial by jury began in England. Under King Henry II, the first juries for a trial were chosen. Slowly, different kinds of juries spread to Europe and to North and South America.

4   Today, a person who knows something special about the crime cannot be a member of the jury. Why do you think this is so?

1. In the United States everyone has the right to
   a. a trial by jury.
   b. bring a sheep into court.
   c. a trial without a jury.
   d. a trial in England.

2. The word in paragraph 1 that means *to make up their minds* or *to settle* is _____.

3. The words "made up of twelve people" in paragraph 1 describe the word _____.

4. The story does not say so, but it makes you think that
   a. jury members steal sheep.
   b. people in England still have trial by jury.
   c. King Henry II did not like boundary lines.

5. In the earliest juries, members were more like
   a. judges.
   b. criminals.
   c. lawyers.
   d. witnesses.

6. People in Japan have the right to a trial by jury.
   Yes   No   Does not say

7. On the whole, this story is about
   a. changing crimes.
   b. changing kings.
   c. changes in trials.

8. What spread to Europe and to North and South America? (Check the story again.)
   a. Different kinds of crimes.
   b. Different kinds of juries.
   c. Different kinds of witnesses.

9. Which of these sentences do you think is right?
   a. People in England have always had trial by jury.
   b. A jury is chosen by the president.
   c. Fair trials came about slowly.

A King and a Queen

1 Termites are small insects that live together in groups. They are called "social insects." Wasps, bees, and ants are the only other social insects.

2 Termites eat wood and live in dark tunnels in trees or underground. Most of the termites in a nest are small males and females without wings. These are the workers. They build the nest and care for the king and queen, the soldiers, and the eggs.

3 The termite soldiers are males and females. They are larger than the workers and have such big jaws that they cannot feed themselves. Food must be put in their mouths by the workers. The soldiers come to any part of the nest that is in danger. To warn the other termites, they bang their heads against the wood and make a loud sound.

4 In a different room in the nest live a little king and a large queen. The queen is sometimes four inches long and very fat. Her only work is laying eggs. From most of these eggs come workers and soldiers. But a few of the eggs become termites with wings. These termites fly off and become the kings and queens of new nests.

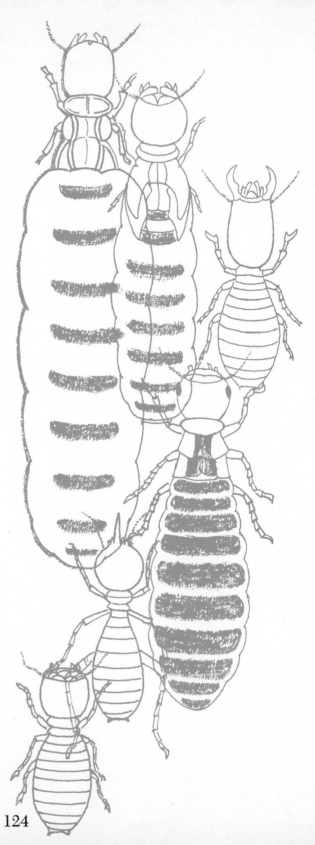

1. Termites live
      a. in caves.   c. in water.
      b. in tunnels.   d. in dens.

2. The word in paragraph 3 that means *to signal* or *to tell someone* is

   _____.

3. The words "they build the nest" in paragraph 2 refer to the

   _____.

4. The story does not say so, but it makes you think that
      a. termites eat other insects.
      b. termites live with wasps, bees, and ants.
      c. termites with wings become kings and queens.

5. Termite soldiers
      a. feed themselves.   c. have large jaws.
      b. are smaller than the workers.   d. are all males.

6. The queen's only job is to lay eggs.
      Yes   No   Does not say

7. On the whole, this story is about
      a. termites as social insects.
      b. kinds of social insects.
      c. underground tunnels.

8. Why do the soldier termites bang their heads against wood? (Check the story again.)
      a. They like the sound it makes.
      b. They are warning other termites of danger.
      c. They are trying to make the nest bigger.

9. Which of these sentences do you think is right?
      a. All termites are alike.
      b. Termites work together as a group.
      c. The termite soldiers do the most work.

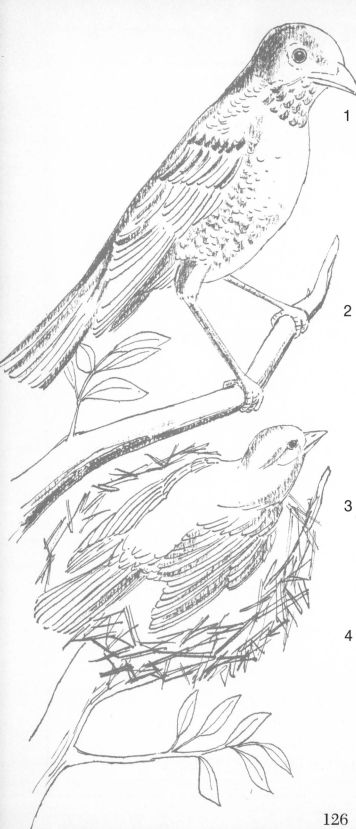

He Saw It First

1   Did you know that birds could be "property owners," too? In the spring, the male robin looks for a place to build a nest. A tree near a green lawn that has many worms suits him best. When he finds the right place, he sings loudly. He tells other birds that this place is his property.

2   At the same time, other birds are choosing places for their nests. A robin does not mind if swallows nest nearby because swallows eat insects. They leave his worms alone. But other robins are different. They would eat the worm supply he needs for his own family.

3   When another male robin comes near, the robin owner sings to warn him away. The property owner looks cross and fierce. He raises his head feathers and holds his tail high.

4   If the owner cannot frighten away the new robin, he attacks. The two fight until one is the winner. The new bird often gives up and flies away. So the first bird has defended his property. He now has the right to build a nest in the place he selected.

1. The male robin looks for a place to build a nest
   a. near swallows.   c. near a lawn with worms.
   b. near other male robins.   d. in the woods.

2. The word in paragraph 1 that means *pleases* or *satisfies* is

   _____ .

3. The words "cross and fierce" in paragraph 3 refer to a robin

   _____ _____ .

4. The story does not say so, but it makes you think that
   a. robins chase away all other birds.
   b. robins do not care where they build their nests.
   c. robins are careful when choosing a place to nest.

5. Robins eat
   a. worms.   c. fruit.
   b. insects.   d. berries.

6. Robins will nest near swallows.
   Yes   No   Does not say

7. On the whole, this story is about
   a. what robins eat.
   b. robins finding a nesting place.
   c. robins finding friends.

8. Why does the male robin raise his head feathers and hold his tail high? (Check the story again.)
   a. He wants to scare away another male robin.
   b. He is getting ready to hunt for worms.
   c. He is too warm.

9. Which of these sentences do you think is right?
   a. The first robin that chooses a tree can build there.
   b. Female robins select the nesting places.
   c. Swallows always help robins defend their property.

The Pecking Order

1   Birds of one kind often stay together in one group, or flock. In every flock, some birds are more important than others. Each bird has its own place. This order goes from the most important to the least important. It is called the "pecking order."

2   In a flock of hens in a barnyard, one hen becomes the most important of the group. She eats first and gets the best perch. She can peck all the other hens. The least important hen is pecked by all the others. She has no other hen to peck. She usually eats last and takes whatever space is left on the perch.

3   To get a place in the pecking order, hens have a pecking contest among themselves. A hen may lose or back away from a fight. Then she becomes less important than the winner and can be pecked by her. Each hen knows which hens to fear and which to peck.

4   Do you have a bird feeder at home or outside your school window? If you do, watch carefully when a group of birds comes to feed. The most important bird in the pecking order will be the first to eat.

1. In every flock of birds,
     a. some are more important.
     b. all are equal.
     c. the males fight the females.
     d. there are many small groups.

2. The word in paragraph 3 that means *a kind of fight* is _____.

3. The words "from the most important to the least important" in paragraph 1 refer to the _____ _____.

4. The story does not say so, but it makes you think that
     a. hens do not fight.
     b. the most important hen can do as she pleases.
     c. hens are the only kind of bird that have a pecking order.

5. The most important hen
     a. eats last.
     b. eats at a bird feeder.
     c. never fights.
     d. gets the best perch.

6. Each bird has its own place in a pecking order.
     Yes   No   Does not say

7. On the whole, this story is about
     a. bird feeders in the barnyard.
     b. flocks of birds in the sky.
     c. the order of birds in a flock.

8. Why do hens have pecking contests among themselves? (Check the story again.)
     a. It is a kind of game that chickens play.
     b. Hens fight to get a place in the pecking order.
     c. They like to have contests.

9. Which of these sentences do you think is right?
     a. Many kinds of birds have pecking orders.
     b. Birds in a flock never fight with each other.
     c. The least important bird must leave the flock.

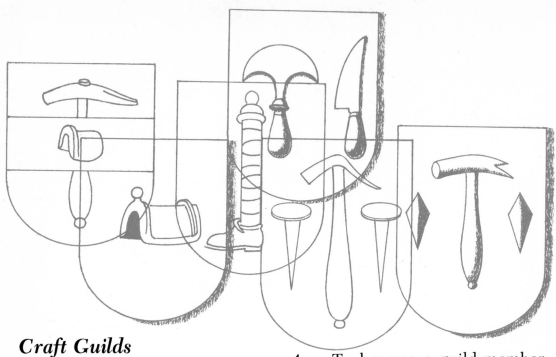

Craft Guilds

1   Today, many people who are skilled at a trade belong to labor unions. As long ago as the Middle Ages, people in western Europe also belonged to a kind of union. These early unions were called guilds.

2   From the 1300s to the 1700s, people who knew a trade joined a craft guild. Guilds were made up of groups of people who did the same kind of work. Shoemakers belonged to the shoemakers' guild. Nail makers belonged to a guild of nail makers.

3   Craft guilds were important in those days. If people were not members of a guild, they could not find work.

4   To become a guild member, a person first had to be an apprentice, or learner. A learner received no pay. Next the person became a journeyman and received pay. At last a person became a master and could open a shop.

5   In the 1800s Candace Wheeler, an artist and maker of American cloth, became interested in women's problems. Many women had good educations but could not earn enough money to live. Candace opened the Women's Exchange, a kind of guild, in New York.

6   At the Exchange women could sell their beautiful handmade dresses and tablecloths. It helped them earn enough to live.

FIND THE ANSWERS

1. Today, many people skilled at a trade belong to
   - a. a shoemakers' guild.
   - b. the Boy Scouts.
   - c. a labor union.
   - d. a group of masters.

2. The word in paragraph 4 that means *a person who is learning a trade* is

   _____.

3. The words "a kind of union" in paragraph 1 describe the word

   _____.

4. The story does not say so, but it makes you think that
   - a. journeymen were very skilled.
   - b. apprentices did not have much money to spend.
   - c. guilds were made up of people who lived in the same town.

5. One kind of union began as long ago as
   - a. the Stone Age.
   - b. the Revolutionary War.
   - c. the Atomic Age.
   - d. the Middle Ages.

6. It was hard for people who were guild members to find work.
   Yes   No   Does not say

7. On the whole, this story is about
   - a. becoming a craft guild member.
   - b. people going on journeys.
   - c. masters who made nails and shoes.

8. Why did people want to belong to craft guilds? (Check the story again.)
   - a. By belonging, they could find jobs.
   - b. They wanted to make shoes and nails.
   - c. They wanted to work where their friends worked.

9. Which of these sentences do you think is right?
   - a. The Women's Exchange sold bread.
   - b. The Women's Exchange sold handwork.
   - c. The Women's Exchange lost tablecloths.

Working Children

1   Almost since time began children have helped their parents at home. In the 1700s, a great change was taking place in England. Cloth and other things which had been made by hand in homes were now made by machines in factories. New inventions caused this change, which was called the Industrial Revolution. Children then began to work outside their homes.

2   Factory owners liked children to work for them. They had small hands and could work the cloth-making machines quicker than an adult. They worked for little money and did as they were told.

3   But the factory owners were often cruel to the children. Five- and six-year-old children were chained to their machines. They often worked as long as 16 hours a day. They did not have nice places to live and were not fed enough. They did not go to school. Sometimes they were taken away from their parents and did not see them again.

4   At last, the government in England began to make laws that helped the children. One of these laws was passed in 1819. It said that children under nine years old could not work in factories. In time, the laws of most countries protected their children.

1. A great change was taking place in England in the
   a. 1400s.   c. 1700s.
   b. 700s.   d. 1800s.

2. The word in paragraph 3 that means *to cause pain or suffering* is

   _____.

3. The words "had small hands" in paragraph 2 refer to the word

   _____.

4. The story does not say so, but it makes you think that
   a. children were kept in cages.
   b. children had many vacations.
   c. few children lived at home.

5. Children often worked as long as
   a. 10 hours a week.   c. 12 hours a month.
   b. 16 hours a day.   d. 20 hours a month.

6. Children who worked in factories had a hard life.
   Yes   No   Does not say

7. On the whole, this story is about
   a. cloth-making machines.
   b. children who worked in factories.
   c. the government of England.

8. Why did the government of England begin to make laws to help children? (Check the story again.)
   a. They wanted the children chained to their machines.
   b. They wanted the children to work for the government.
   c. They wanted the children to be treated better.

9. Which of these sentences do you think is right?
   a. Children liked to work in factories.
   b. Children who worked in factories lived with their parents.
   c. At one time, children did much of the factory work.

Labor Unions

1 The Industrial Revolution brought great changes in both England and the United States. Many workers were needed to work the new machines. People from the country went to the cities to find jobs in factories.

2 Sometimes these factory workers were not well treated. Their working days were very long. Their pay was small. The bosses did not listen to the demands of one or two workers. In America, the workers began to band together into groups called "labor unions." These groups were the first unions in the world.

3 A labor union could demand better working conditions. If its demands were not met, the people in the union would not work. They went "on strike" until they had what they wanted.

4 At first, unions were small groups in their own cities. If they had strikes that did not work, the unions fell apart. Next, all the unions in a city grouped together. All the people in all the unions were able to help one another.

5 At last, unions from all over the country banded together into very large groups. Then the unions were a more powerful group. People felt that they had help when they asked for better working conditions.

1. The new machines of the Industrial Revolution needed
   a. many workers.   c. no repairs.
   b. new parts.   d. too much oil.

2. The word in paragraph 2 that means *to get together in groups* is

   _____.

3. The words "people in the union would not work" in paragraph 3

   explain the words _____.

4. The story does not say so, but it makes you think that
   a. labor unions were formed to help one or two workers.
   b. people on strike did not belong to a union.
   c. the United States had labor unions before other countries.

5. Labor unions are found
   a. just in the country.   c. nowhere.
   b. just city-wide.   d. all across the country.

6. People who were not in the unions could not get what they demanded.
   Yes   No   Does not say

7. On the whole, this story is about
   a. cities.
   b. the growth of labor unions.
   c. working conditions in factories.

8. Why did so many people find jobs in factories? (Check the story.)
   a. The factories paid their workers a lot of money.
   b. New machines made many more jobs open to workers.
   c. They didn't like to live in the country.

9. Which of these sentences do you think is right?
   a. Labor unions helped people get better working conditions.
   b. Workers have always had short hours and high pay.
   c. Union members never go on strike.

A Big Post Office

1   A post office in a large city is a busy place. Big machinery helps to move the mail to the right place in the building.

2   Large sacks of mail slide along a moving belt. Baskets full of packages roll by. Letters run through a machine that "looks at" them to see if they have a stamp. The machine moves very fast. It can "look at" 20,000 letters in one hour.

3   The noise and excitement do not bother Helen De Liere, who works in the post office at Inglewood, California. Helen is deaf. Because she can neither speak nor hear, Helen gives all her attention to her job.

4   She likes to sort letters. She looks at the zip code numbers that tell her where a letter is to go. Then she puts the letter in the right box for Chicago or Denver.

5   Helen also runs a machine that sorts letters for her. It looks like a typewriter. A letter slides into place. Helen looks at the zip code and pushes a button. The letter slides out and into the Denver box of mail. It is faster than sorting by hand.

6   Helen works so hard that the post office wants more workers like her. Other workers are learning sign language so they can talk to Helen.

1. A post office in a large city is
        a. hot.   c. crowded.
        b. busy.   d. dusty.

2. The word in paragraph 3 that means *to trouble or disturb* is

    _____.

3. The words "can 'look at' 20,000 letters in one hour" tell about a

    _____.

4. The story does not say so, but it makes you think that
        a. people in small towns do not get mail.
        b. a large post office needs many workers.
        c. firemen help sort the mail.

5. To sort letters, Helen looks at the
        a. stamp.   c. mail truck.
        b. typewriter.   d. zip code.

6. All letters are sorted by hand.
        Yes   No   Does not say

7. On the whole, the story is about
        a. driving a mail truck.
        b. learning sign language.
        c. a large post office.

8. Why doesn't noise bother Helen? (Check the story.)
        a. Helen is deaf.
        b. Helen likes noise.
        c. Helen cannot see.

9. Which of these sentences do you think is right?
        a. Letters do not need stamps.
        b. Large post offices use machinery to help.
        c. Deaf people cannot work.

A Small Post Office

1   The first postmaster of Baltimore, Maryland, was Mary Katherine Goddard. Today, 200 years later, and a few miles away, there is another woman postmaster. She is Irene Cannon. All her clerks are also women.

2   The post office is in the town hall of Glen Echo, Maryland. The seven women who work there are friendly and helpful. They tie packages, answer questions, and weigh parcels. People who come to mail letters do not hurry away. Often, they like to stay and talk to the clerks.

3   Irene and her clerks work hard, but they also like to make their work fun. On holidays such as Christmas or Valentine's Day they decorate the post office from top to bottom.

4   In December the clerks put up a big Christmas tree and hang candy canes all around. Sometimes, one of the women will dress as a Christmas angel. On the Fourth of July, she might dress as Betsy Ross or Martha Washington.

5   Would you like to buy a stamp from Betsy Ross?

1. Mary Katherine Goddard was the first postmaster of
   a. Chicago.   c. Baltimore.
   b. New York.   d. New Orleans.

2. The word in paragraph 2 that means *wrapped packages* is

   _____.

3. In paragraph 2 the words "friendly and helpful" refer to

   _____.

4. The story does not say so, but it makes you think that
   a. women like to sing.
   b. women are good postal workers.
   c. women cannot mail letters.

5. Glen Echo post office is decorated
   a. in red, white, and blue.   c. at night.
   b. on holidays.   d. in the winter.

6. The Glen Echo post office is in the town hall.
   Yes   No   Does not say

7. On the whole, this story is about
   a. Christmas trees.
   b. Baltimore.
   c. A small post office.

8. In December, what do the clerks put up? (Check the story.)
   a. Shamrocks.
   b. A Christmas tree.
   c. Flags.

9. Which of these sentences do you think is right?
   a. Glen Echo has a woman postmaster.
   b. Betsy Ross lives in Glen Echo.
   c. Glen Echo has no post office.

Brown Bag Bank

1 In 1975 a different kind of bank opened in New York City. It is called the First Women's Bank. Madeleine McWhinney was its first president.

2 Women not only save their money at this bank, they also get help on the best way to spend it. One woman may want to know if she should buy a stereo this year. The bank people might tell her to save a little more money before she buys it. Another woman may want to sell her farm. The bank people might tell her how much money it is worth.

3 Many people liked the idea of a bank for women. In 1976, an-other women's bank was opened in San Diego, California. This bank has a special service. It is called the "brown bag" service.

4 The bank people in San Diego hold a class during lunch hours to help men and women learn more about banking. The men and women may bring their lunches with them in brown paper bags. They eat while they are learning. That is why it is called the "brown bag" service.

5 Other women's banks will soon open in many cities in the United States. Maybe your city will have one, too.

1. In 1975 a different kind of bank opened in
   a. New York City.   c. Pittsburgh.
   b. Hollywood.   d. Omaha.

2. The word in paragraph 1 that means *head of a company or a government*

   is _____.

3. The words "hold a class during lunch hours" in paragraph 4 refer to

   the _____.

4. The story does not say so, but it makes you think that
   a. there are not many women's banks in this country yet.
   b. there are no banks in San Diego.
   c. banks are open at night.

5. A woman may want to sell her
   a. stereo.   c. farm.
   b. house.   d. furniture.

6. There is a Women's Bank in St. Paul.
   Yes   No   Does not say

7. On the whole, this story is about
   a. women's lunches.
   b. women's banks.
   c. women's cars.

8. When does the San Diego bank hold classes? (Check the story.)
   a. In the summer.
   b. In October.
   c. During lunch hours.

9. Which of these sentences do you think is right?
   a. Women's banks are a big help to women.
   b. Nobody likes women's banks.
   c. Women's banks do not help men.

Buildings from the Past

1   Many people visiting the South-west stop at Santa Fe, New Mexico. There, they see long, low buildings that have flat roofs. Most houses are only one story high. They have beautiful small gardens with walls around them.

2   The buildings are tan and brown like the earth because they are made of adobe (ə dō′ bē). Adobe is a Spanish word that means "sun-dried brick." It is made by mixing clay soil, straw, and water. Its cost is low. Houses built of adobe stay cool in the summer heat and warm in winter.

3   Santa Fe is one of the oldest cities in North America. About 1610, Spanish settlers gave Santa Fe its name. Centuries before the Spanish came, the Pueblo (pweb′ lō) Indians lived there. The city's adobe buildings are much like those the Indians lived in long ago. The gardens are like those built by the early Spanish settlers.

4   The people of Santa Fe liked their early Spanish-American buildings. So they passed a law in 1953. It said that all new buildings in the older part of town had to look like the adobe buildings. Now a part of Santa Fe will remind people of the city's long history.

FIND THE ANSWERS

1. In Santa Fe, New Mexico, there are many
    a. Japanese buildings.   c. English gardens.
    b. adobe buildings.   d. pointed roofs.

2. The word in paragraph 4 that means *to help someone remember some-thing* is _____.

3. The words "sun-dried brick" in paragraph 2 describe the word

    _____.

4. The story does not say so, but it makes you think that
    a. Santa Fe has never changed its name.
    b. adobe is a new kind of brick.
    c. the Indians built many gardens.

5. Santa Fe was named by
    a. the Pueblo Indians.   c. Spanish settlers.
    b. visitors.   d. the government.

6. People make their own adobe bricks.
    Yes   No   Does not say

7. On the whole, this story is about
    a. North American gardens.
    b. Spanish-American laws.
    c. adobe buildings in Santa Fe.

8. Why did the people of Santa Fe pass a law about adobe buildings? (Check the story again.)
    a. There were too many people living in new buildings.
    b. They wanted to make the city modern.
    c. They wanted one part of town to stay the same.

9. Which of these sentences do you think is right?
    a. The people in Santa Fe are proud of their city's history.
    b. The people in Santa Fe like modern buildings.
    c. Pueblo Indians are the only people who live in Santa Fe.

The Town That Woke Up

1 In 1699 the governor of Virginia made plans for a new capital for his colony. The new capital city was called Williamsburg. It was built with wide streets and beautiful houses. The buildings and governor's home were the finest in the colony. Williamsburg was a busy place until 1780. Then the capital was moved to Richmond, and Williamsburg went to sleep.

2 When the capital moved, the people moved away, too. The old houses began to need paint, roofs caved in, and gardens became thick with weeds.

3 Almost 150 years later, John D. Rockefeller, Jr., became interested in the town. He gave money to re-build Williamsburg just as it had been. In 1926 work began.

4 Rockefeller's wife, Abby Aldrich Rockefeller, liked American folk art. When the town was rebuilt, Mrs. Rockefeller gave her collection of early American paintings and dolls to a museum there.

5 Today, the homes and gardens look as they did when the town was new. Many people dress as people dressed long ago. They make shoes and candles, as people did in the past. Thousands of people visit Williamsburg each year. They see a beautiful American town of two centuries ago. It is the town that woke up.

1. Williamsburg is in the state of
   - a. New York.
   - b. Richmond.
   - c. Virginia.
   - d. America.

2. The word in paragraph 1 that means *the city where the head of the government is found* is _____.

3. The words "wide streets and beautiful houses" in paragraph 1 refer to the word _____.

4. The story does not say so, but it makes you think that
   - a. much money is needed to rebuild a town.
   - b. Williamsburg is now the capital of our country.
   - c. few people visit Williamsburg.

5. When Williamsburg was built, its streets were
   - a. filled with weeds.
   - b. wide.
   - c. caved in.
   - d. in need of paint.

6. Williamsburg is a new American city.
   Yes   No   Does not say

7. On the whole, this story is about
   - a. John D. Rockefeller, Jr.
   - b. people moving away.
   - c. Williamsburg, Virginia.

8. Why did the people leave Williamsburg after 1780? (Check the story again.)
   - a. They ran out of food.
   - b. The town was burned to the ground.
   - c. The capital was moved to Richmond.

9. Which of these sentences do you think is right?
   - a. Williamsburg helps visitors learn about early America.
   - b. The capital of Virginia is Williamsburg.
   - c. Thousands of people live in Williamsburg.

Make-Believe Towns

1   The movie cowboy is being chased by a band of Indians. The horse gallops through the streets of an old Western town.

2   Chances are that the cowboy is not riding through a real town! The buildings probably have false fronts and no backs. The town is a movie set.

3   Most movie studios keep one or more "towns" on the studio grounds. Someday, you may visit a movie studio. Then you can see these sets. There is the old Western town with its sheriff's office and general store. There is a small midwestern town that has a church and town hall. Walking down the streets of another set, you may think you are in a large city.

4   The buildings on a set must fit the time and place of the movie being filmed. Perhaps a movie's story is supposed to take place in a New England town of the 1800s. The people who make sets must take time to learn what such a town would be like. They study books and pictures. They make a trip to a real New England town. The set must not look like a make-believe town. It must look true to life.

FIND THE ANSWERS

1. The people who make sets study
   - a. other sets.
   - b. churches and town halls.
   - c. books and pictures.
   - d. studio grounds.

2. The word in paragraph 2 that means *not real* is _____.

3. The words "it must look true to life" in paragraph 4 refer to a

   _____.

4. The story does not say so, but it makes you think that
   - a. many movies are not filmed in real towns.
   - b. most movies take place in small midwestern towns.
   - c. it is easy to build make-believe towns.

5. Buildings on a set often are
   - a. Indian teepees.
   - b. books and pictures.
   - c. real towns.
   - d. false fronts.

6. People can visit movie studios.
   Yes   No   Does not say

7. On the whole, this story is about
   - a. sets made by movie studios.
   - b. movies that are filmed in large cities.
   - c. cowboys and Indians.

8. Why do people who make sets go to real towns? (Check the story.)
   - a. They like to travel to different places.
   - b. They want to see how to make sets look real.
   - c. They get tired of make-believe towns.

9. Which of these sentences do you think is right?
   - a. All movie studios have dozens of sets.
   - b. You can tell when you see a movie with a make-believe set.
   - c. When you see a movie, the buildings in it look real.

Our Polluted Water

1 We must have water to live. If the water we use is not clean and fresh, it can make us ill. The animals that live in and around lakes and rivers must also have clean water.

2 Our rivers and lakes supply most of our water. The clear, blue water found by the first American settlers has changed. Many of our water sources now are polluted. They are filled with dirt and waste which cannot be cleaned out. In many places, water is not safe for most uses.

3 Lake Erie was once a beautiful lake. Now it has been called "a dying lake." Waste from nearby homes and factories has been dumped into it. Fish can no longer live in much of its polluted water.

4 George Washington once called the Potomac "the finest river in the world." Now its water is no longer blue. Instead, it is a "soupy green." Suds, from detergents used to wash clothes, often cover the water of our rivers.

5 Water cannot be made in a factory. Once water is polluted, it is hard to make it clean and safe. We must learn to take care of the water we now have.

FIND THE ANSWERS

1. Most of our water supply comes from
   a. oceans.
   b. wells.
   c. springs.
   d. rivers and lakes.

2. The word in paragraph 2 that means *dirty* or *not safe to use* is

   _____.

3. The words "a dying lake" in paragraph 3 refer to

   _____.

4. The story does not say so, but it makes you think that
   a. we have an endless supply of fresh water.
   b. all kinds of life need fresh, clean water.
   c. polluted waters are beautiful.

5. Our rivers are often polluted by
   a. detergents.
   b. fish.
   c. rocks.
   d. lakes.

6. It is easy to make polluted water safe again.
   Yes   No   Does not say

7. On the whole, this story is about
   a. polluted water.
   b. washing clothes.
   c. going fishing.

8. We must learn to take care of the water we now have because
   a. factories need time to learn how to make water.
   b. we must have water to use in the future.
   c. the first settlers used up most of the water.

9. Which of these sentences do you think is right?
   a. Water pollution is a problem today.
   b. Our water is still clean and safe.
   c. Suds from detergents help clean polluted water.

Clean or Dirty Air?

1   In a large American city not long ago many paintings were damaged by "bad" air. In New York City in 1966, 168 people died and thousands became ill from fumes in the air.

2   Air pollution, or dirty air, is caused by many things. Great clouds of smoke come from factory chimneys. Cars send smoke and fumes into the air. Burning waste fills the air with bits of dirt. Even burning leaves add smoke to the air.

3   Sometimes, airplanes cannot find their landing spots through the smoke. Smoke of all kinds is bad to breathe and can do great harm to the body.

4   Still, we cannot live without air. We must find a way to clean the air we have.

5   In time, we may have factories that are run by atomic energy. Our cars may run on smoke-free electric power. Scientists are also working on new ways to keep the oil burned by cars from making fumes. Waste may be buried in the sand on ocean floors.

6   These changes might keep our air clean in the years to come. But until then, many scientists are looking for ways to make air cleaner now.

1. Scientists are now working on ways to
   - a. make new paintings.
   - b. keep airplanes from flying.
   - c. bury sand on ocean floors.
   - d. stop air pollution.

2. The word in paragraph 1 that means *gas* or *smoke* is _____.

3. The words "dirty air" in paragraph 2 describe

   _____ _____.

4. The story does not say so, but it makes you think that
   - a. stopping air pollution is hard.
   - b. dirty air is blown away by the wind.
   - c. airplanes cannot fly through smoke.

5. Air pollution is caused by
   - a. clouds.
   - b. ocean floors.
   - c. smoke and fumes.
   - d. paintings.

6. Works of art have been damaged by dirty air.
   Yes   No   Does not say

7. On the whole, this story is about
   - a. dirty air.
   - b. electric power.
   - c. burning oil.

8. Why would electric cars cut down on air pollution? (Check the story again.)
   - a. They go only a short way.
   - b. They are easier to keep clean.
   - c. Electric power has no smoke.

9. Which of these sentences do you think is right?
   - a. Ways to stop pollution must be found.
   - b. Air is clean.
   - c. It is good for our lungs to breathe smoke.

America's Changing Face

1   Almost a thousand years ago, the first explorers landed on America's shores. Deep forests grew everywhere they looked. Birds and animals filled the skies and the forest floor.

2   In time, the forests were cleared. People needed wood to build new houses and buildings, so they cut down the trees. The early settlers killed many animals for food.

3   Farmers soon learned that hillside soil could not be used for farming. Rain washed away the rich soil. So the farmers let their cattle eat the new grass as it came up. But too many animals fed there. All the grasses were soon gone, and the soil became bare. Now much land cannot be used for either farming or grazing.

4   Our country's forest areas are often badly treated. Not long ago, several Boy Scouts picked up 30 pounds of trash along a forest path.

5   The face of our land has changed. The sides of our roads are often covered with trash dropped by careless people. More trees and animals are destroyed each year. But if we learn to take care of what is left, we can keep America beautiful.

152

1. When the first explorers landed in America, they found
   a. trash.   c. cattle.
   b. forests.   d. settlers.

2. The word in paragraph 3 that means *eating grass* is _____.

3. The words "are often badly treated" in paragraph 4 tell about

   _____ _____.

4. The story does not say so, but it makes you think that
   a. forests are no longer needed.
   b. our forests were not always used in a wise way.
   c. there are no more forests in the United States.

5. The early settlers cut down trees to
   a. build houses.   c. make paths.
   b. grow grass.   d. find birds and animals.

6. Trees and animals are destroyed every year.
   Yes   No   Does not say

7. On the whole, this story is about
   a. Boy Scouts picking up paper.
   b. farming on hillside soil.
   c. taking care of our trees and animals.

8. What happened after cattle ate the hillside grass? (Check the story again.)
   a. The birds had no place to hide.
   b. The soil became bare.
   c. The hillsides were turned into farming land.

9. Which of these sentences do you think is right?
   a. Trash dropped by people makes America beautiful.
   b. If people really tried, they could keep America beautiful.
   c. Animals no longer live in forests.

Twenty-Three Cents a Word

1   On the dark, cold floor of the Atlantic Ocean are several black cables. They stretch from the United States to Europe. Each cable looks like a thick garden hose. Inside the cables are wires carrying messages at a speed of 400 words per minute. If you wish, you can send a message to England for twenty-three cents a word.

2   By 1856 there were telegraph wires on land, but there were none that crossed an ocean. An American, Cyrus W. Field, believed that telegraph wires could be laid on an ocean bottom. The wires could be put inside a thick cable.

3   Men on British and American ships tried to put down the first Atlantic cable. They had many troubles. The cable broke again and again.

4   Field did not quit. In 1866 a new cable worked perfectly. Today, many undersea cables carry messages around the world.

5   Sometimes it is hard to lay telephone cables, too. The ground may be rocky or hilly. Then a telephone company may put up a microwave tower. People like Marie Stanley of Southwestern Bell Company check the spot where this radio tower will go. When it is built, the tower can carry long-distance messages cheaper and with less noise than a telephone cable makes.

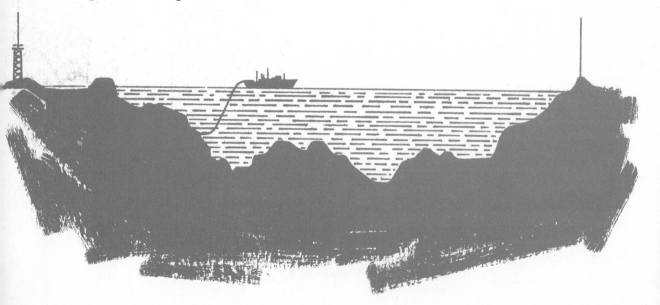

1. Wires in the Atlantic cables carry messages at a speed of
   a. 20 words per minute.   c. 10 words per second.
   b. 400 words per minute.   d. 20,000 words per hour.

2. The word in paragraph 1 that means *to reach from one place to another*
   is _____.

3. The words "broke again and again" in paragraph 3 refer to the word
   _____.

4. The story does not say so, but it makes you think that
   a. the telegraph is older than the cablegram.
   b. undersea telegraph wires were put inside thick garden hoses.
   c. it took a big ship twenty years to lay the cable.

5. The Atlantic Ocean floor is
   a. full of rocks.   c. warm and muddy.
   b. cold and dark.   d. colorful and bright.

6. It was easy to lay the first undersea cable.
   Yes   No   Does not say

7. On the whole, this story is about
   a. the life of Cyrus W. Field.
   b. life on the floor of the Atlantic Ocean.
   c. the first Atlantic cable.

8. Why did Cyrus W. Field want to lay a cable across the Atlantic? (Check
   the story.)
   a. He wanted to send a message to India.
   b. He believed he could send messages across the ocean.
   c. He wanted to travel across the Atlantic in a ship.

9. Which of these sentences do you think is right?
   a. Cables under the Atlantic carry messages only to England.
   b. Today, undersea cables are no longer used.
   c. Undersea cables have been in use for more than 100 years.

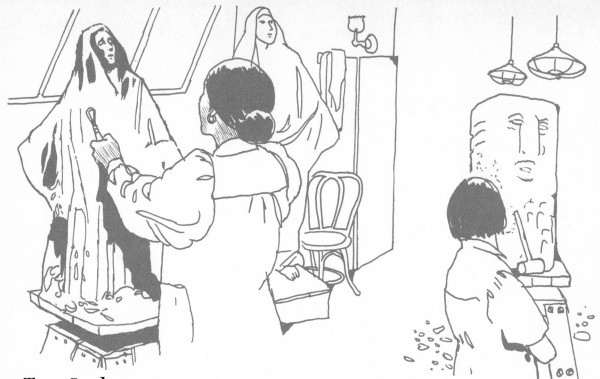

Two Sculptors

1   Have you ever made a turtle or an elephant out of clay? This is the way many sculptors begin work on a large statue. They make a small model out of clay. Then they follow the same lines as they carve or mold their large pieces.

2   Sculptors often carve things they see around them. This might be a person or an animal. Some carve figures that show feeling, such as sorrow or happiness. Still others carve figures that tell of an idea, such as "power."

3   Marina Núñez del Prado, a famous sculptor of Bolivia, liked to make statues of figures from Bolivian Indian stories. Her work reminds us of long ago times.

4   Edmonia Lewis was a sculptor from New York. She had a black father and an Indian mother. Her Indian name was *Wildfire*. Edmonia wanted her statues to show feelings.

5   One of her statues is called *Hagar in the Wilderness*. Hagar, a woman of the Bible, and her son were forced to wander in the desert. Hagar's face looks tired and sad. People who look at Edmonia's statue understand how all women felt who have suffered.

6   Can you think of a statue that shows an idea?

FIND THE ANSWERS

1. Marina Núñez del Prado is a famous
   - a. teacher.
   - b. soldier.
   - c. sculptor.
   - d. artist.

2. The word in paragraph 1 that means *people who make statues* is

   _____.

3. The words "a woman of the Bible" in paragraph 5 refer to

   _____.

4. The story does not say so, but it makes you think that
   - a. many good sculptors are women.
   - b. sculptors always make statues of people.
   - c. all sculptors live in New York.

5. Sculptors' models are often made of
   - a. stone.
   - b. wood.
   - c. clay.
   - d. sand.

6. Edmonia Lewis's Indian name was *Wildfire*.
   Yes   No   Does not say

7. On the whole, this story is about
   - a. American Indians.
   - b. the Bible.
   - c. two sculptors.

8. How does Hagar's face look? (Check the story.)
   - a. Sunburned.
   - b. Pleased.
   - c. Tired and sad.

9. Which of these sentences do you think is right?
   - a. Sculpture is an art form.
   - b. Clay statues will last forever.
   - c. Nobody makes statues of animals.

Invisible Messages

1   It would be difficult to imagine a world without radio. Some of us even carry small radios in our pockets. Before radio, the best way to send messages a long way was by wire.

2   By 1838, Samuel F. B. Morse had invented a working telegraph. He had also invented a new alphabet made up of dots and dashes. This alphabet was called Morse Code.

3   The telegraph uses electricity and wire. Messages in Morse Code could go only where there were telegraph wires.

4   Scientists knew that radio waves moved through the air. They believed that radio messages could be sent without wires. No one knew how to do it.

5   The man who found a way to send wireless messages was Guglielmo Marconi (gü lyel′ mō mär kō′ nē) of Italy. His first signals went only a few miles, but he wanted to send messages across the Atlantic Ocean. Marconi went to Newfoundland to try to receive signals from England.

6   Late in 1901, the letter "S" was sent out in Morse code from England. "Dot, dot, dot" came the signal. Marconi picked it up on his set.

7   In a short time, wireless was in use everywhere. Americans call it radio. It can send invisible messages around the world.

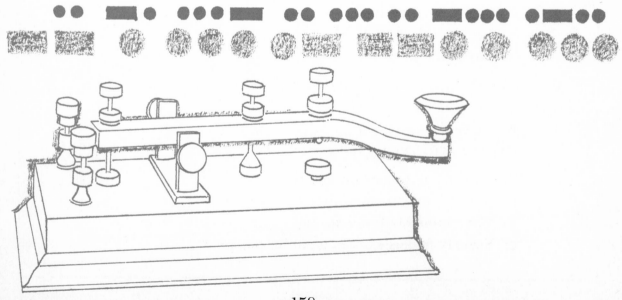

1. A working telegraph was invented by
   a. Guglielmo Marconi.   c. Thomas A. Edison.
   b. Samuel F. B. Morse.   d. George Washington.

2. The word in paragraph 7 that means *cannot be seen* is

   _____ .

3. The words "a new alphabet made up of dots and dashes" in paragraph 2

   refer to the _____ _____ .

4. The story does not say so, but it makes you think that
   a. telegraph messages are sent to a satellite.
   b. radio messages can be sent where telegraph messages cannot.
   c. wireless messages can go only a few miles.

5. Marconi wanted to send wireless messages
   a. to a satellite in space.   c. across the Atlantic Ocean.
   b. to the moon.   d. to Samuel F. B. Morse.

6. Radio waves move along wires.
   Yes   No   Does not say

7. On the whole, this is a story about
   a. scientists and alphabets.
   b. England, Italy, and Newfoundland.
   c. the telegraph and the radio.

8. Why was the wireless important? (Check the story again.)
   a. Wire could be used in other ways.
   b. Radio messages could be sent where there were no wires.
   c. Wireless changed the alphabet.

9. Which of these sentences do you think is right?
   a. The wireless made sending messages quicker.
   b. Morse and Marconi worked together on the wireless.
   c. Radio waves cannot be sent without wires.

Taboos

1   There are certain things that people think they must not do. These are called taboos. People who have a taboo act in a certain way. They think that to act differently would bring bad luck. Some people think that walking under a ladder will bring bad luck.

2   For the people of one tribe in Africa, it was taboo to count anything. If people wanted to know how many goats they had, they looked quickly. Then they guessed how many goats were there. They thought something bad would happen to the goats if they counted them.

3   For another tribe in Africa, it was taboo to talk about the misfortune of an ancestor. These people thought the ancestor's spirit would hear them and become angry. Then the spirit would punish them.

4   Saying their own names was taboo for Polar Eskimos. They believed evil spirits were always listening when they spoke. It would not be safe to say their names out loud. Evil spirits would cause bad luck. If someone asked, "Who is there?" an Eskimo would answer, "It is I." Eskimos would never give their names.

1. For Polar Eskimos it was taboo to
      a. walk under a ladder.
      b. say their names.
      c. talk to anyone.
      d. count anything.

2. The word in paragraph 1 that means *to do* or *to behave* is

   _____.

3. The words "certain things that people think they must not do" in

   paragraph 1 tell about the word _____.

4. The story does not say so, but it makes you think that
      a. everyone should walk under ladders.
      b. goats bring bad luck.
      c. different peoples have different taboos.

5. One tribe in Africa believed that they should not
      a. speak to spirits.
      b. listen to others.
      c. ask questions.
      d. count their goats.

6. Polar Eskimos live in tribes.
      Yes   No   Does not say

7. On the whole, this story is about
      a. the weather in Africa.
      b. the clothes of a Polar Eskimo.
      c. taboos among different peoples.

8. Why wouldn't Polar Eskimos say their names out loud? (Check the story.)
      a. They couldn't remember their names.
      b. They believed that their ancestors would hear them.
      c. They thought it would bring bad luck.

9. Which of these sentences do you think is right?
      a. Taboos are something to eat.
      b. Many peoples have taboos.
      c. Evil spirits are always listening to what you say.

From Page to Knight

1   During the Middle Ages in England, all boys from important families were expected to become knights. But first, they had to learn many things.

2   When a boy was seven, he was sent to a friend's castle. There, he started his training as a page. He began by doing all kinds of small tasks. He also learned to ride a horse. He had to do his work well and without a fuss.

3   After seven years, a page became a squire. As a squire, he learned to use weapons and to hunt. In time, he could fight beside his master in battle.

4   When they were twenty-one, squires who had done well were made knights in long, serious ceremonies. Sometimes a squire became a knight after he had been very brave in battle. Then the ceremony was quick. The squire's master might say, "I hereby make you a knight." To finish the ceremony, the master gave the new knight a slap on the shoulder or the cheek.

5   All knights had to promise certain things. They promised to tell the truth and to be brave. They had to be kind to women and children. Above all, they promised to serve God and their king.

1. A page learned to
   - a. fight in battle.
   - b. use weapons.
   - c. make a fuss.
   - d. ride a horse.

2. The word in paragraph 4 that means *special acts for special times* is

   _____.

3. The words "learned to use weapons and to hunt" in paragraph 3 refer

   to a _____.

4. The story does not say so, but it makes you think that
   - a. all boys did not become knights.
   - b. a page had a lot of free time for play.
   - c. pages did not know how to ride a horse.

5. Knights promised to
   - a. be brave and kind.
   - b. fight and hunt.
   - c. be a page.
   - d. own a castle.

6. The ceremony of a squire becoming a knight was always quick.
   Yes   No   Does not say

7. On the whole, this story is about
   - a. boys in America.
   - b. girls in the Middle Ages.
   - c. becoming a knight.

8. How did a squire become a knight? (Check the story again.)
   - a. He talked to the king about it.
   - b. He took part in a special ceremony.
   - c. He slapped himself on the cheek.

9. Which of these sentences do you think is right?
   - a. It took many years of hard work to become a knight.
   - b. Knights did not have to follow rules or keep promises.
   - c. Knights became kings.

Eskimo Good Manners

1   You say "please" when you ask someone for something and "thank you" when you get it. You are using good manners. Polar Eskimos had their own ways to show good manners.

2   Polar Eskimos liked to visit with one another. When Eskimos had good hunting, they put aside the best meat to serve guests. Then they invited the other families in the community to dinner. While visiting, both the Eskimo host and the Eskimo guests used good manners.

3   The Eskimo hosts were eager to be thought good hosts. Being good hosts made Eskimos important in the community. The hosts served the best meat. However, it would have been bad manners to say so. It was good manners for them to say they wished they could have served better. The hosts said they did not hunt well and that their meat was not good.

4   The guests then used their good manners. They told the hosts they were great hunters. They said the food was the best anywhere. They made noises to show how much they enjoyed the food. They ate until they could not eat another bite.

1. Eskimos like to
    a. live alone.
    b. use bad manners.
    c. be good hosts.
    d. serve tough meat.

2. The word in paragraph 3 that means *neighborhood* or *area* is

    _____.

3. The words "used their good manners" in paragraph 4 refer to the

    _____.

4. The story does not say so, but it makes you think that
    a. Eskimos do not like meat when it is cooked.
    b. Eskimo life is very different from ours.
    c. Eskimos are unfriendly to each other.

5. When Eskimo families visited one another,
    a. everyone used good manners.   c. they just talked.
    b. they ate a little snack.   d. they sat around a fire.

6. Being a good host made an Eskimo important in the community.
    Yes   No   Does not say

7. On the whole, this story is about
    a. the Middle Ages.
    b. how to be a great hunter.
    c. good manners among the Polar Eskimos.

8. Why did Polar Eskimos invite other families to dinner? (Check the story.)
    a. They had so much meat that they couldn't eat it all.
    b. They didn't want to be alone.
    c. They liked to visit with friends.

9. Which of these sentences do you think is right?
    a. Good manners are different in different places.
    b. Eskimos are bad hunters.
    c. The Polar Eskimos do not like to have guests.

The Noodlehead and the Pumpkin
(A Persian Folktale)

There was once a strong young man who was a great wrestler. He lived alone in the woods near the small village of Hums.

The wrestler was as strong as a bear. Sometimes, just for fun, he pulled up hundred-year-old trees by the roots.

Now, the people of Hums were so stupid that they were called Noodleheads. Of all the people in Hums, the wrestler was the most stupid.

One day, the wrestler decided to go to the city. "Maybe I can find someone who will wrestle with me," he said. And he started out.

Hums was a tiny town, and the wrestler had never seen many people before. When he came to the city, he saw hundreds and thousands of people. He was afraid that he would get lost.

"Suppose I forget who I am?" he thought. "I couldn't find myself in these crowds."

The wrestler saw a man selling pumpkins. He bought the biggest pumpkin he could find. He tied it by a string to his right leg. He could not get lost now! He walked along, dragging the pumpkin.

"Good day," said a young man. "Where do you come from?"

"I come from Hums," said the wrestler.

The young man knew that Hums was the home of the Noodleheads. "Why do you have a pumpkin tied to your leg?" he asked.

"There are so many people here that I might not know who I am," said the wrestler. "As long as I have a pumpkin tied to my leg, I know that I am I. When it is time to leave, I'll know that I am the one who goes home to Hums."

"Come home with me," said the young man. He thought it would be fun to play a trick on this stupid Noodlehead. "Be my guest for awhile," he said.

"Thank you," said the wrestler, and he followed the young man to his home. They ate a good dinner and went to bed. As soon as the wrestler was asleep, the young man took the pumpkin from the wrestler's leg and tied it on his own.

Early the next morning, the wrestler awoke. The pumpkin was gone! He went to find his new friend. He saw a young man who was still asleep with a pumpkin tied to one leg.

The wrestler rubbed his head. It felt like his head, but how could it be? He could see that he was still in bed. "How wise I was to buy that pumpkin!" he said to himself. "There I am asleep, and I thought I was awake! If that's the wrestler, then I'm the man who owns this house."

He went outside and sat on a rock. "This city is no place to live," he decided. "I've heard that Hums is the best place to live. I think I'll go there." He looked at the fine house. "I guess I'll sell it," he said.

Soon a man and his wife came by. They were carrying heavy loads of furniture. Behind them came seven children.

The wrestler felt sorry for them. "May I help you carry something?" he asked.

"I'm looking for a house to buy," said the man.

"You have come to the right place," said the wrestler. "This house is for sale."

The man took a bag from his pocket. "All the money I have is this bag of gold," he said.

"That will be fine," said the wrestler. He took the gold and started to leave. Then he remembered something.

"Inside your house you will find a man with a pumpkin tied to his leg," said the wrestler. "He won't stay long. He's a Noodlehead." And the wrestler went home to Hums.

618 words

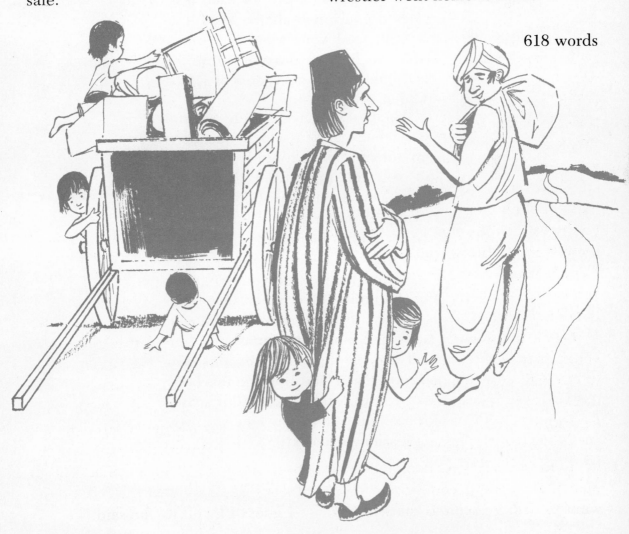

169

KEEPING CHARTS ON SKILLS

Fill in your record chart after each test. Beside the page numbers, put a one for each correct question. Put zero in the box of each question you missed. At the far right, put your total. Nine is a perfect score for each test.

When you finish all the tests in a concept, total your scores by question. The highest possible score for each question in one concept is the number of stories.

When you have taken several tests, check to see which questions you get right each time. Which ones are you missing? Find the places where you need help. For example, if you are missing Question 3 often, ask for help in learning to use directing words.

As you begin each concept, copy the chart onto lined paper. Down the left side are the test page numbers. Across the top are the question numbers and the kinds of questions. For example, each Question 1 in this book asks you to recall a fact. Your scores for each question show how well you are learning each skill.

Your Reading Scores

Concept I

Question	fact	vocabulary	modification	inference	fact	confirming content	main idea	cause and effect	inference	Total for Page
	1	2	3	4	5	6	7	8	9	
Page 15										
17										
19										
21										
23										
25										
27										
29										
31										
33										
35										
37										
39										
41										
43										
45										
47										
49										
51										
53										
55										
57										
59										
61										
Totals by question										

Your Reading Scores

Concept II

Question	fact	vocabulary	modification	inference	fact	confirming content	main idea	cause and effect	inference	Total for Page
	1	2	3	4	5	6	7	8	9	
Page 67										
69										
71										
73										
75										
77										
79										
81										
83										
85										
87										
89										
91										
93										
95										
97										
99										
101										
103										
105										
107										
109										
111										
113										
Totals by question										

Your Reading Scores

Concept III

	fact	vocabulary	modification	inference	fact	confirming content	main idea	cause and effect	inference	Total for Page
Question	1	2	3	4	5	6	7	8	9	
Page 119										
121										
123										
125										
127										
129										
131										
133										
135										
137										
139										
141										
143										
145										
147										
149										
151										
153										
155										
157										
159										
161										
163										
165										
Totals by question										

WORDS YOU WILL NEED

These are words and names that are hard to read. Learn how to say each word. Find the word in the story. Learn the meaning. Use the word in a sentence of your own. The words are only listed once. You will need the words you learned to read the stories that follow.

p. 14
force
invention
later
spears
stirrups
toes
Asia
Chinese
India

p. 16
borrowed
evergreens
inventions
recent
science
special
waterfall
China
Japan
Japanese
Korea

p. 18
alphabet
alphabetic
centuries
easily
manner
traders
travels
Mediterranean Sea
Phoenicia
Phoenicians

p. 20
beetle
dragonfly
mantis
scoop
stinger

stun
victims
wasp

p. 22
moss
motions
sly
spiders
webs

p. 24
echoes
ink-black
ledge
oilbirds
owl-like
South America

p. 26
longer
modern
projects
tribe
Africa

p. 28
exporting
famous
grown
importing
industry
products
steel-making
Canada
Europe
Holland
Netherlands
North Sea

p. 30
communities
reservations

smaller
themselves
travel
wealth
Arizona
Navaho Indians
New Mexico
Spaniards
Utah

p. 32
band-aid
jello
language
photo
photograph
scotch
smog
English
Mexico
Sandwich
Turkey

p. 34
chat
example
foreign
per
probably
spoken
syllables
television
throughout
vocabulary
French
German
Katze

p. 36
announcers
automobile
flicks
flyover

freight
hooter
overpass
pronounce
subway
telly
underground
England
Queen's English

p. 38
colorful
curving
decorate
decoration
designs
imaginations
palm
Middle East
Mohammed
Moslems
Persia

p. 40
ceremonies
cowhide
materials
medicine
watercolors
Southwest

p. 42
canoes
cedar
decorated
easier
objects
totem
well-known
wooden
Alaska
Haida

Northwest
Canada

p. 44
outsiders
searching
stone-tipped
Arunta
Australia
Stone Age

p. 46
materials
medical center
stadium
turban
Doña Fela
Doña Felisa Rincón Del Gautier
Puerto Ricans
Puerto Rico
San Juan

p. 48
calendars
central
enemies
fibers
hammock
tribes
tropics
villages
Brazil

p. 50
century
pyramids
rafts
sloping
Egypt
Great Pyramid
Greeks
King Cheops

p. 112
entire
ourselves
scars
Nubas
Sudan

p. 114–116
gobbled
parrot
polite
raisins
sidewise

p. 118
castes
create
religious
warriors
Aryans

p. 120
afford
collects
Colonial
education
property
usually
Massachusetts

p. 122
boundary
crime
earliest
guilty
jury
trial
witnesses
Europe
King Henry II

p. 124
females
social
termites
wasps

p. 126
defended
fierce
selected
supply
swallows

p. 128
carefully
contest
perch
whatever

p. 130
apprentice
craft
education
employer
guilds
journeymen
labor
makers
skilled
unions
Candace Wheeler
Middle Ages
Women's Exchange

p. 132
adult
Industrial
Revolution

p. 134
conditions

p. 136
excitement
typewriter
zip code
Chicago
Denver
Helen De Liere
Ingelwood,
California

p. 138
decorate

parcels
postmaster
Baltimore,
Maryland
Betsy Ross
Glen Echo,
Maryland
Irene Cannon
Martha Washington

p. 140
stereo
First Women's Bank
Madeleine McWhinney
San Diego,
California

p. 142
adobe
North America
Pueblo Indians
Santa Fe,
New Mexico
Spanish

p. 144
capital
collection
colony
governor
lawmakers
museum
Abby Aldrich
Rockefeller
John D.
Rockefeller, Jr.
Richmond
Virginia
Williamsburg

p. 146
Midwestern
sheriff's
someday
studies
studios
Indians
New England

p. 148
detergents
polluted
sources
suds
George
Washington
Lake Erie
Potomac

p. 150
atomic
breathe
energy
fumes
pollution
scientists
New York City

p. 152
areas
careless
explorers
trash
Boy Scouts

p. 154
cables
microwave
tower
perfectly
stretch
telegraph
undersea
Atlantic Ocean
Cyrus W. Field
Marie Stanley
Southwestern
Bell Company

p. 156
model
mold
sculptor (s)
statue
wander
Bolivia

Edmonia Lewis
Hagar in the
Wilderness
Marina Núñez
del Prada
Wildfire

p. 158
difficult
electricity
invisible
receive
signals
wireless
Guglielmo
Marconi
Newfoundland
Samuel F. B.
Morse

p. 160
ancestor
differently
misfortune
polar

p. 162
castle
fuss
hereby
knights
serious
squire

p. 164
community
invited
manners
Eskimos

p. 166–169
awoke
dragging
stupid
wrestler
Hums
Noodleheads

7 8 9 10 VHVH 86 85 84 83 82

176